AMERICA IS
IMMIGRANTS

AMERICA IS IMMIGRANTS

★

Sara Nović

ILLUSTRATED *by*

ALISON KOLESAR

RANDOM HOUSE

New York

For my grandmother,
and her mother.

—S.N.

For my husband, all four of whose
grandparents were immigrants.

—A.K.

CONTENTS

CONTENTS

CONTENTS

CONTENTS

EXPLORERS

CONTENTS

THINKERS

—

INTRODUCTION

Whenever I'm considering what something means to me, I try to think about it outside the bounds of English. If a language carries culture within it, then our perspectives invariably shift with the words we use. I am lucky to have a few languages through which to sift, and with a concept as vast and varied as *America*, I needed all the help I could get.

American Sign Language (ASL) is perhaps better suited than most to shed light on exactly what Americanness means. A melding of French, Old Kentish, Martha's Vineyard, homemade, and possibly Native American signed languages in nineteenth-century Connecticut, it is a language that offers a diverse and homegrown glimpse of how Americans see themselves.

There are lots of different folk etymologies about the nature and origin of the ASL word *America*. Some say the intertwined fingers mirror the corners of a log cabin, or an agreement between many states in the union. Others point to the sign's circular motion as a reference to the stirring of a melting pot.

Meanwhile, the movement in the word *immigrant* is thought to mimic the wavy blue lines across a green-card or passport stamp.

Linguistically, the four- and five-finger handshapes used in both signs frequently function as classifiers representing large groups of people.

Like any language, ASL often isn't iconic, and there's limited research about what these signs' concrete origins could be. But for me—a linguaphile if certainly no linguist—the similar handshapes in *America* and *immigrant* strike a powerful image. Like the sign itself, America is built on immigrants intertwined, its foundations reliant on the strength of the place where they interlock.

A M E R I C A

Growing up, I understood my own family's history and traditions to be rooted elsewhere, or at least transplanted here from away. But rather than being at odds with our Americanness, this was what *made* us American. Here we could hold tight to, but also mix and match and interweave, the languages, music, and food we most loved. It's this space, more than any display of military, economic, or technological might, where America's best chance at being truly exceptional lies.

WHO'S IN THIS BOOK?

There are 193 member states in the United Nations; this book contains at least one person from each of them. Several nations, including the Holy See, Palestine, Kosovo, Taiwan, and Tibet, that face ongoing political questions of sovereignty but do have a degree of recognition from members of the international community are also featured here. While not all the individuals in this book are U.S. citizens, they've spent a significant amount of time living, working, and learning here, and have all impacted the nation for the better.

IMMIGRANT

WHO'S FROM WHERE?

What started out feeling like a much tidier project than a novel soon collapsed into a complicated exploration of identity and history. The people I'd begun researching were born in one place but identified ethnically with another. And countries are not constant. They appear and vanish from the globe, leaving those who were born and raised there without guidance as to what they now might call home. While a political battle over a border wall raged around me, I amassed living proof of the artificiality, injustice, and utter subjectivity of borders all across the world.

How can you define a person's background? By her birthplace? Her parents'? Her language? The answer, it seems, is different for different people. Wherever possible, I've deferred to the ethnicity and nationality by which a person identifies themselves.

America is immigrants, but it isn't *only* immigrants. You'll find two extremely significant groups—Native Americans and enslaved people—largely absent from this book. This is not because their impact on the country wasn't vast and deserving of attention, but because including them under the banner of "immigrants" is out of keeping with the goal of honoring people's choices in self-identification.

Native American history is American history, and indigenous people's contributions to modern American science, medicine, and culture are numerous, ranging from popcorn and chewing gum to syringes and baby formula. But Native Americans aren't immigrants; evidence for human life in the Americas goes as far back as forty thousand years, and many Native origin stories, like that of the Navajo, clearly identify Native Americans as indigenous to the continent. Out of respect for these oral histories, I have not included Native people in this book.

So much of American migration hinges on agency, and the

search for freedom and opportunity. To refer to enslaved people as immigrants would be to ignore their loss of agency, to strip away the trauma and terror of their experience. However, the profound impact of slavery, enslaved people, and the rich cultures they brought with them from Africa cannot be ignored. To this end, I've written briefly about the Middle Passage and Great Migration on page 3. While it cannot do justice to the experience of enslaved people, I hope it will at least serve as a moment's pause, lest we forget how very American an institution slavery was.

On the individual level, there are so many immigrants worthy of recognition who do not appear in this book. While I tried to feature a wide variety of lives and achievements, this project is in no way exhaustive. Instead, I hope this book can be a springboard from which readers can continue to learn about the people who make their communities, cities, and country so special.

AMERICA IS
IMMIGRANTS

ON ENSLAVED PEOPLE

Africa to North America from the 1500s to 1865

★

Kidnapped and taken thousands of miles from their homes, chained, degraded, and sold, they were not immigrants.

The Middle Passage, the three-to-four-month journey along the African coast and across the Atlantic Ocean, was harrowing and deadly. It's estimated that 15 to 30 percent of those who were abducted died during the coastal march. At sea, the enslaved people were imprisoned belowdecks with little water and no space to move around—10 to 15 percent of them would not reach land again.

Those who survived the passage, an estimated 10.5 million people, were further stripped of their humanity and condemned to lives of forced labor and abuse. Enslaved people's experience of the Americas was the opposite of everything colonists claimed the place represented—a chance at a new life, a safe harbor for freedom.

Nevertheless, the ugly truth of the slave trade is at the very core of America's foundations. By 1840 more than half of the country's exports were produced by enslaved labor. Enslaved people built large swaths of the American railroad system, the Capitol Building, Wall Street, and the White House, as well as many of the nation's prized banks, churches, and universities.

American culture, too, was shaped by enslaved people, and after emancipation that influence exploded. Scholar Isabel Wilkerson likens the experience and impact of the Great Migration, in which six million African Americans migrated north of the Mason-Dixon Line, to more Eurocentric ideas about immigration.

Black people in the South were "Americans who had to act like immigrants in order to be recognized as citizens," Wilkerson said in an interview with *On Being*. "They were forced to seek political asylum within the borders of their own country."

As dynamic as the impact of any immigrant wave, the Great Migration further infused the nation with the languages and traditions carried through those first abhorrent journeys across the Atlantic.

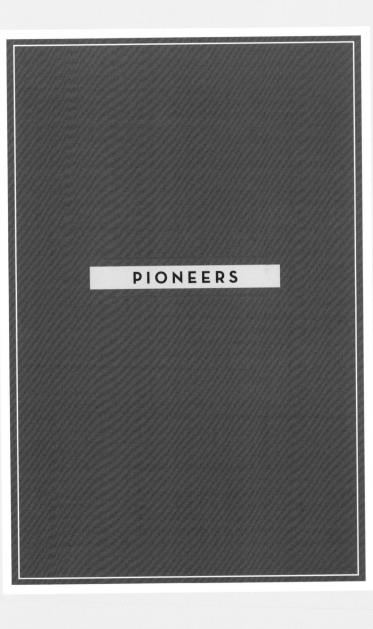

PIONEERS

DESI ARNAZ

Migrated from Cuba circa 1933

★

One of America's most beloved television couples almost wasn't.

When executives approached starlet Lucille Ball about adapting her popular radio show for TV, she insisted her real-life husband, Desi Arnaz, be her co-lead. CBS was opposed to a Latino man playing the husband of an all-American redhead, but the couple wouldn't budge. When executives relented, the television classic *I Love Lucy* was born.

By some accounts, Ball and Arnaz were TV's first interracial couple; undoubtedly they were the first bicultural one. Arnaz's character, Ricky Ricardo, was designed to upend stereotypes: He was a successful businessman, and the rational one of the pair. Arnaz's heritage was a focus of the show, but not as fodder for cheap jokes; only Lucy was allowed to mimic his accent.

Arnaz was also an innovative producer. He and his crew developed the multicamera setup that allowed for recording on adjacent sets in front of a live audience, a system that would become widely used in television production. Arnaz negotiated to retain the rights to the show's content so that he and Ball could advocate for, control, and profit from syndication. Because of this, Arnaz is considered the inventor of the rerun, and he and Ball became the first-ever TV-actor millionaires.

The rest is history—xenophobic concerns about Americans' ability to connect with a Cuban lead were all for naught. On January 19, 1953, the episode "Lucy Goes to the Hospital" drew more viewers than the inauguration of President Eisenhower the next day. Over half a century later, the show's reruns continue to delight television audiences.

Arnaz, who had arrived in the States as a teenage refugee, today has two stars on the Hollywood Walk of Fame.

KATHLEEN "KAY" MCNULTY

Migrated from Ireland in 1924

★

Before she programmed computers, she was a computer. One of about a hundred women employed by the army as human "computers" during World War II, Kay McNulty calculated missile trajectories. The work was painstaking; each weapon had its own firing table, each table had about 1,800 trajectories, and every trajectory took about thirty to forty hours of hand calculations.

The slow pace of progress on a single table meant turnover was high, but McNulty had always had a knack for numbers and didn't find the job tedious. She'd arrived in the States as a young girl when her father, imprisoned for his affiliation with the Irish Republican Army, moved the family to Philadelphia upon his release. At the time McNulty knew only Gaelic but went on to excel in school and become one of three women in Chestnut Hill College's class of 1942 to graduate with a degree in mathematics.

In an effort to speed up computation processes, engineers developed the ENIAC, one of the earliest computers. The media dubbed the eight-by-eighty-foot behemoth the "Giant Brain," but few understood its power. McNulty was one of six women chosen to program the ENIAC.

With no set programming language, the women invented and wrote programs out on cards, then physically input them into the ENIAC's panels by hand via cables and switches. At the time, none of them knew they were performing calculations toward the development of the hydrogen bomb.

As with many women's roles during World War II, the contributions of McNulty and her colleagues were forgotten to such an extent that recent historians who came across a photo of women beside the ENIAC believed they had been placed there as models. The lack of acknowledgment, though, didn't bother McNulty, whose interests in recognition lay closer to home. "If I am remembered at all, I would like to be remembered as my family storyteller," she said.

TECH WIZARDS

Today, most Americans can't imagine their daily lives without computers, cellphones, or the Internet. Many of the apps and websites we use every day were created by immigrants.

ANDREW GROVE (HUNGARY) A co-founder of Intel, he served as the company's CEO, COO, and president, and was *Time* magazine's 1997 Man of the Year for his contributions to "the growth in the power and the innovative potential of microchips."

JERRY YANG (TAIWAN) Knowing only the word *shoe* in English when he arrived in San Jose, California, he went on to co-found Yahoo and organize the venture capital firm AME Cloud Ventures.

SERGEY BRIN (RUSSIA) The co-founder of Google and current president of Google's parent company, Alphabet Inc., he's one of the world's top twenty richest people.

MAX LEVCHIN (UKRAINE) A co-founder of PayPal, he was particularly focused on fraud protection systems, including an early iteration of today's CAPTCHA technology.

STEVE CHEN (TAIWAN) A former employee of PayPal and Facebook, he co-founded YouTube, now part of Google.

JAN KOUM (UKRAINE) He co-founded WhatsApp, a Wi-Fi-based messaging platform popular for international communications, now owned by Facebook.

LUIS VON AHN (GUATEMALA) An early pioneer of CAPTCHA security challenge questions, crowdsourcing, and human computation methods, he co-founded the popular language-learning app Duolingo.

RUS YUSUPOV (TAJIKISTAN) Inventor of the short-form video-looping social media tool Vine, he co-founded Intermedia Labs and is the COO of HQ Trivia, a live game-show app.

CHRISTINA QI (CHINA) In 2014, while an international student at MIT, she founded with friends in her dorm Domeyard LP, a hedge fund company that creates custom software for high-frequency trading. Today, Domeyard does $1 billion in trades each day.

SIDNEY POITIER

Migrated from the Bahamas in 1942

★

At first, Sidney Poitier was an accidental American. His parents, tomato farmers on Cat Island, Bahamas, traveled often to Miami by sailboat to sell their produce, and it was on one such trip that he was born, more than two months premature. It was 1927, and he was not expected to survive, but the family returned to the Bahamas a few months later with a healthy baby boy.

He had no formal education. When he was ten, his family moved to Nassau, where he saw his first car, glass windows, running water, and electricity. It was also the first time he saw a motion picture.

At fifteen he returned to Miami to live with his brother, but fled to New York City after a run-in with the KKK. He auditioned for the American Negro Theatre and was rejected for his thick accent and poor reading skills. Working as a dishwasher, he asked a waiter at the restaurant to help him practice reading the newspaper. He spent hours mimicking radio newscasters to reduce his accent.

He returned to the American Negro Theatre and was again rejected, but did janitorial work in order to take classes, eventually squeezing himself into an understudy position. When one night a play's star, Harry Belafonte, didn't show, Poitier took the stage. A director who happened to be in the audience invited him to audition for an upcoming Broadway show. Poitier was nineteen.

Eighteen years later, he would become the first black person and the first Bahamian to win an Academy Award for Best Actor, for his role in *Lilies of the Field*. Poitier recently told the American Academy of Achievement's *What It Takes* podcast that one of his life's big regrets was not being able to find the waiter who'd taught him how to read.

MONA MAY KARFF

Migrated from Moldova via Palestine in 1930

★

If life imitates chess, seven-time U.S. women's chess champion Mona May Karff was a well-protected queen. Shrouded in mystery, so little was known about her origins that the United States Chess Federation listed her birthplace only as "Europe."

Karff was born in Bessarabia, a Russian territory most of which is known as Moldova today. Her father taught her to play chess before she'd reached double digits, and soon she was beating him and other challengers with ease. Of Jewish ancestry, she and her family moved to Tel Aviv, where she dominated the local tournament-chess scene.

She set out for the United States at age twenty-one and was briefly married to her cousin. Karff was so quiet about her past that even her best friend didn't know she had been married until nearly half a century later, though a subsequent long-term relationship with U.S. Open chess champion Edward Lasker was common knowledge.

In 1950, she was one of the first American women to be named International Woman Master, but even the limelight couldn't reveal much about her life beyond the board. She sometimes called herself by the initial *N*, but refused to explain where the *N* had come from. Friends knew only that she traveled widely for tournaments and pleasure, spoke eight languages, and liked art and opera. After her death it was discovered that, while not a queen, she was sitting on a small fortune: A talented stock market investor, she'd amassed millions and a large art collection from the comfort of her Manhattan apartment without anyone noticing.

TAMMY DUCKWORTH

Migrated from Thailand in the 1980s

★

The only thing stronger than the titanium prostheses on which she stands is Duckworth's mental fortitude; a combination of bravery, honesty, and ambition has made the junior senator from Illinois a force to be reckoned with on Capitol Hill.

No surprise that her strength has fashioned her a woman of firsts: Among the first army women to fly combat missions during Operation Iraqi Freedom, she also became the war's first female double amputee. Less than a decade later, she'd be elected the first Thai-born and first disabled woman in Congress.

Born in Bangkok to a Thai mother and American father, Duckworth hails from a long tradition of American military service. Ancestors on her father's side have fought in every major American conflict since the Revolutionary War; her father, Franklin Duckworth, was a Marine Corps captain who served in World War II and the Korean War.

Duckworth is unequivocal about using her life experiences to further her platform. "I had my legs blown off in Iraq, and because I had my legs blown off in Iraq, people are listening to me," Duckworth told *The New York Times* with her usual candor. "I'm not going to get my legs back, and that's fine, but if that gives me a platform to talk about the things that are important to me, like education and jobs, that's great."

In 2018, Duckworth also became the first sitting U.S. senator to give birth. As a result, the Senate changed its rules to allow babies younger than one on the floor so Duckworth could continue to cast votes during her maternity leave. Sharing an image of her daughter's debut outfit—a duckling onesie and accompanying jacket—she joked about whether the look would comply with the Senate's policy requiring blazers.

ERNEST LYON (BELIZE) A member of the Republican National Committee starting in 1896, he served as U.S. ambassador to Liberia from 1903 to 1910 under President Theodore Roosevelt.

FELIX FRANKFURTER (AUSTRIA) One of the founders of the American Civil Liberties Union and an adviser to Franklin D. Roosevelt, he served on the Supreme Court from 1939 to 1962.

HENRY KISSINGER (GERMANY) A Jewish refugee from Nazi Germany, he served as national security adviser and then secretary of state under Presidents Richard Nixon and Gerald Ford.

ELIAS ZERHOUNI (ALGERIA) He was appointed director of the National Institutes of Health by President George W. Bush in 2002. During his tenure, the NIH tripled its international funding for global health. Under Barack Obama's administration, he became an ambassador encouraging scientific collaboration among nations.

JIM YONG KIM (SOUTH KOREA) The president of the World Bank from 2012 to 2019, he founded the international healthcare nonprofit Partners in Health. He was president of Dartmouth College from 2009 to 2012, the first Asian American to serve as president of an Ivy League school.

WILMOT COLLINS (LIBERIA) A refugee of the First Liberian Civil War, he beat the four-term incumbent to become mayor of Helena, Montana, in 2017, and became the first black person to be elected mayor anywhere in Montana since statehood.

PREET BHARARA (INDIA) The former U.S. attorney for the Southern District of New York, he became known for tackling corruption and crimes of money laundering, insider trading, and Ponzi schemes on Wall Street.

JESSIE RODRIGUEZ (EL SALVADOR) As a child, she and her family fled to the United States during El Salvador's civil war. The first Latina Republican to serve in the Wisconsin state legislature, she was sworn into the state assembly in 2013.

RAFFI FREEDMAN-GURSPAN (HONDURAS) Adopted as a young child and raised in Massachusetts, she became the country's first openly transgender White House staffer, serving under President Obama as outreach and recruitment director of the Presidential Personnel Office, White House LGBT liaison, and United States Holocaust Memorial Council member.

JERRY SPRINGER

*Of Polish descent; migrated from the
United Kingdom in 1949*

★

As the host of a talk show, catapulted to fame by sensationalizing everyday people's family dramas, Jerry Springer has a birth story to match his brand: He was born underground in a London tube station. It was 1944, the Nazis were conducting their "Baby Blitz" bombing campaign, and Highgate's tube stop had been transformed into a civilian bomb shelter. Springer's parents were Jewish refugees who'd recently fled Poland. His grandmothers were both killed in concentration camps.

His early life and résumé offered no hints at what would ultimately be the source of Springer's celebrity. His family moved to the States when he was a young boy, and he had a quiet childhood in Queens. He studied political science at Tulane and got his law degree at Northwestern. He was a political adviser to Robert F. Kennedy's presidential campaign, and won a spot on Cincinnati's city council when he was just twenty-seven. He'd go on to become the city's well-loved mayor in 1977.

When he was cast as the host of *The Jerry Springer Show* in 1991, the program was supposed to be a political-issues talk show. Only after a ratings-inspired makeover did it become what its twenty-seven-season run was famous for being: a showcase of outlandish family secrets, revealed amid a heaping dose of cursing and brawling. By 1998, the show had tied the reigning *Oprah Winfrey Show* in viewership.

For Springer, the transition from do-gooder mayor to scandalous talk show host did not seem strange. "Showbiz, politics, and law all have something in common," he told *The Jewish Chronicle*. "You're selling something." For his next act, Springer will offer up another amalgam of his skills as the host of the 2019 courtroom show *Judge Jerry*.

JERRY SPRINGER

LEA SALONGA

Migrated from the Philippines circa 1990

★

When Disney released *Aladdin* in 1992, the animated-movie empire was just starting to experiment with complex female characters, pushing beyond helpless cookie-cutter princesses to create women with minds of their own. Jasmine was one of those early models, a rare Disney woman who maintains agency for most of the film, tells it like it is to her father, and is willing to eschew wealth and power for love and independence.

Before she became the singing voice of Jasmine's whole new world, Lea Salonga had already broken down barriers in the entertainment world. In 1991 she was the first Asian actress to win a Tony Award, for her performance as Kim in Broadway's *Miss Saigon*. The next year, Salonga was right back on stage making more history; the first Asian woman to play Éponine in *Les Misérables*, she'd later return to the show's revival to play Fantine.

By the time Salonga returned to Disney in 1998, the company had made further strides in developing its female leads. Fa Mulan was the first Disney princess who wasn't a princess at all. She spends the majority of the film in combat and dressed as a man in order to protect her father. Salonga lent her voice to the famed ballad "Reflection," in which Mulan struggles with society's expectations for young women—a far cry from the company's Snow Whites and Sleeping Beauties. In 2011, Salonga was named a Disney Legend, honored for her contributions to transforming the film industry at a time when Asian women were largely ignored.

Salonga divides her time between the United States and the Philippines, where she continues to embody the fight for women's independence off-screen, advocating for women's access to healthcare and contraception.

DAVID HO

Migrated from Taiwan in 1965

According to David Ho, much of life is left to chance. As a college student, he read a book about blackjack and learned to count cards. While some consider gambling a waste of intellect, and casinos object to card counting as giving an unfair advantage, Ho just sees it as a measuring of possibilities. "I would rather call it an exercise in probability and statistics," he told the Academy of Achievement.

By that definition, it was chance, too, that led him to enter the field of HIV and AIDS research. Arriving in the United States at age twelve with no knowledge of English, Ho would go on to excel at school, studying at the California Institute of Technology and Harvard Medical School. He was a resident at UCLA when he encountered some of the first patients infected with what was not yet known as AIDS.

"I was at the right place at the right time, having just finished the right type of training, getting ready to do the right type of training that would be relevant to this problem," he said. "Chance does play a very, very important role. . . . We have to be prepared to take advantage of the opportunities that are bubbled up by serendipity."

But it is through hard work, not luck, that Ho and his team have since made several transformative discoveries in the field: They were the first to understand the virus's carrier state, a period where patients are symptomless but the virus remains dynamic. His understanding of the virus's replication mechanism led to the development of the antiretroviral and protease inhibitor medications that effectively treat the disease today. Ho also noticed that HIV behaves differently in the lab than in the body of an infected host, clearing a key hurdle in the development of a vaccine, his ultimate goal. He's currently testing antibodies he believes could definitively neutralize the virus.

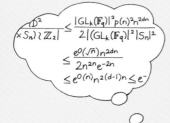

$$\frac{D^2}{\times S_n) \wr \mathbb{Z}_2|} \leq \frac{|GL_k(\mathbb{F}_q)|^2 p(n)^2 n^{2dn}}{2|(GL_k(\mathbb{F}_q)|^2 |S_n|^2}$$

$$\leq \frac{e^{O(\sqrt{n})} n^{2dn}}{2n^{2n} e^{-2n}}$$

$$\leq e^{O(n)} n^{2(d-1)n} \leq e^{-}$$

HALLOWED OLAOLUWA (CENTRAL AFRICAN REPUBLIC) The youngest African-born person ever to earn a doctorate, he's now conducting mathematical physics research at Harvard University. His current work has future implications for thermodynamics, optics, computer science, and complex, multivariable budgeting for large-scale systems (like an entire nation's government).

RAYMOND WANG (CANADA) At age seventeen, he won the world's largest student science fair for creating a device that prevents the spread of microbes and disease through airplane cabins. The ventilation system is designed to retrofit existing airplanes, and could be installed in just one day. Wang is currently an undergraduate at Harvard.

ZANDILE "PEPE" SIBANDZE (ESWA-TINI, FORMERLY SWAZILAND) Working as a housekeeper in South Africa, she surprised her boss by fixing his broken pool pump herself rather than calling out for repairs. Learning that she was passionate about flight, he helped her get a job at an airport, where she could earn enough money to pay for high school. She's currently a student at Embry-Riddle Aeronautical University in Florida, likely the first woman from Eswatini to study aerospace engineering.

ANURUDH GANESAN (INDIA) Growing up, he heard stories of how his grandparents had carried him ten miles to a clinic to be vaccinated, only to arrive and find the vaccines spoiled for lack of refrigeration. As a high schooler, he turned heads at Google's and the White House's science fairs with his transportation system that keeps vaccines at a stable temperature without ice or electricity. He's currently an undergraduate at the University of Pennsylvania.

LEONARD AND PHIL CHESS

Migrated from Poland (now Belarus) in 1928

★

In the late 1940s, African American musicians and record companies were worlds apart: While blues and the beginnings of rock and roll were burgeoning in the African American community, white-owned record companies wouldn't give the musicians a second glance, hiring white artists to re-create sanitized versions of popular "race records." But for brothers Leonard and Phil Chess, the blues felt natural. "We'd been around it all our lives," Phil Chess once told *Vanity Fair*. "We came from Poland in 1928. That was blues all the time."

Born Lejzor and Fiszel Czyż, the brothers were Polish Jews who arrived in Chicago at ages eleven and seven, and grew up working in their father's junkyard. The two showed entrepreneurial spirit early on, opening a liquor store and then a nightclub on the city's predominately African American South Side.

Eventually they bought a stake in Aristocrat Records, the company they'd take over and transform into Chess Records. They'd planned to enter the jazz world and had little technical knowledge of the blues as a genre. Nevertheless, they were intrigued by the song "I Can't Be Satisfied," and made it their first release. The musician, unknown at the time, would turn out to be the father of modern Chicago blues, Muddy Waters. The record sold out in two days.

Chess Records provided a platform for some of the most important African American artists of the century, introducing Chuck Berry, Willie Dixon, Howlin' Wolf, and Etta James to mainstream audiences. Chess musicians would form the bedrock of American R&B and rock and roll and were cited as influences on the many rock and pop stars who covered these icons' music for the rest of the century. The brothers were inducted into the Blues Hall of Fame in 1995.

MARIA BORGES

Migrated from Angola in 2012

★

She is, like all the best models, a shape-shifter. One moment looking severe in a large, bejeweled nose ring for Givenchy, the next jubilant in Moschino's floor-length red and blue flapper fringe. Dapper in a khaki suit and oversized tie for Giorgio Armani, then sultry in the iconic white angel wings of Victoria's Secret.

But her aesthetic flexibility is nothing compared to her physical and mental versatility. Maria Borges was born in Luanda, the capital of Angola—a country ravaged by a decades-long civil war. She was eleven years old when her mother died. Her older sister, then sixteen, became her caretaker and guardian.

She arrived in America as a teenager after finding encouragement and representation at a modeling contest in Angola, and promptly became a frontrunner in the field, booking seventeen shows in her first fashion week. In 2013, she was part of the first group of black models ever to walk in a Christian Dior show. In 2015, she was the first black model to walk in a Victoria's Secret show with her natural hair, a short, curly Afro. In 2017, she was the first African woman to make the cover of *Elle* in the twenty-first century.

The mantra "step by step" inked along the side of her arm is one thing about her look that doesn't change, a reminder of something her sister used to say in times of uncertainty. "One step for Angola, one step for New York," Borges said of the tattoo in an interview with *Vogue*. "My dream is to be a top model. I want to be number one in the world. It won't happen fast. I have to go one step at a time."

MADELEINE ALBRIGHT

*Migrated from Czechoslovakia
(now the Czech Republic) in 1948*

★

International relations were her lived experience, her family legacy, and her distraction of choice.

Madeleine Albright was Jewish but didn't know it. Her parents converted to Catholicism and took the family to the United Kingdom as the Nazis invaded Czechoslovakia. They never told their children about their heritage; Albright would learn only decades later, as she stepped onto the international stage, that three of her grandparents had died in concentration camps.

Beneath a metal kitchen table, four-year-old Madeleine weathered the Blitz on the outskirts of London. After the war, her family moved to Yugoslavia, her father serving as the Czech ambassador to the nation. But when the family arrived on Ellis Island via the SS *America* in 1948, it was to seek political asylum; her father had been ousted from his post by Czechoslovakia's new Communist government.

Albright's father went on to become a popular professor of international relations. "I tried to pattern myself after him," she told the *Los Angeles Times.* When she married and gave birth to premature twins, she began taking Russian lessons as a distraction from their hospitalization. Slowly, she earned her PhD in public law and government while raising her three daughters.

Albright would go on to become the U.S. ambassador to the United Nations, then the first female secretary of state, under President Bill Clinton. Known for broadcasting her opinions via bejeweled brooches on her suit lapels, she was a strong advocate for democracy and interventionism. The roots of her commitment to these values are easy to see when looking back on her life. She was outspoken about the need for U.S. involvement in Rwanda, Haiti, and particularly, in Bosnia during the breakup of Yugoslavia, one of the many places she'd called home.

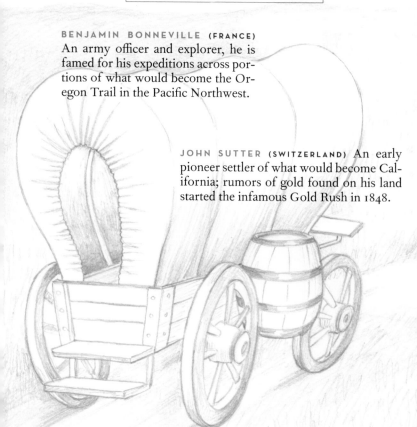

BENJAMIN BONNEVILLE (FRANCE)
An army officer and explorer, he is famed for his expeditions across portions of what would become the Oregon Trail in the Pacific Northwest.

JOHN SUTTER (SWITZERLAND) An early pioneer settler of what would become California; rumors of gold found on his land started the infamous Gold Rush in 1848.

ANTHONY FRANCIS LUCAS (CROATIA)
Salt and oil miner; his drilling of the Texas oil field Spindletop in 1901 ushered in the petroleum age.

GEORGE COMER (CANADA) A whaler, polar explorer, and early anthropologist, he made multiple Arctic and Antarctic voyages in the late 1800s, and studied Inuit art and culture.

FINN RONNE (NORWAY) On multiple early-twentieth-century expeditions of the South Pole, he photographed thousands of miles of Antarctic coastline. He also worked on U.S. naval operations to establish Antarctic bases and complete the mapping of the continent.

GEORGE DOUMANI (PALESTINE) His extensive geologic research helped prove the theory of continental drift. Two Antarctic mountains are named for him.

BUILDERS

ALEXANDER HAMILTON

Migrated from St. Kitts and Nevis in 1772

★

This Founding Father was an illegitimate son. He was denied membership in the Church of England, and education in the church school, because his parents weren't married. He arrived in the colonies an orphaned, penniless teenager with no formal education. John Adams would describe him as "the bastard brat of a Scottish peddler."

His origins a constant source of embarrassment, Alexander Hamilton was known for the chip on his shoulder and a fiery temper, due in large part to being unpracticed in the social mores of the wealthy and well-educated classes he would first encounter as a scholarship student at King's College (now Columbia University).

But his humble beginnings also bred legendary ambitions. Hamilton would prove himself indispensable to General George Washington in the Revolutionary War and then to the nation, co-authoring *The Federalist Papers* to promote the ratification of the Constitution, founding the *New York Post*, and eventually becoming the nation's first secretary of the treasury.

Self-made and largely self-educated, Hamilton had no qualms about looking everywhere for new ideas, and he founded his economic policy on pieces of the best systems he saw around the world, creating a federal tax system and establishing the nation's credit internationally.

Having an orphan boy in charge of all the country's money rubbed many vying for power the wrong way, but Hamilton's success in crafting the inner workings of a brand-new economic powerhouse came because, not in spite, of his life's struggles, making him perhaps the earliest achiever of what would come to be known as the American dream.

NIKOLA TESLA

Ethnically Serbian; migrated from the
Austrian Empire (now Croatia) in 1884

★

He was born at midnight in a summer storm, lightning blazing through the village of Smiljan. The midwife declared the weather a bad omen, predicting Nikola Tesla would be a child of the storm. "No," was his mother's fabled reply. "Of light."

A polyglot with a photographic memory, Tesla dropped out of university and was hired by the Edison company to work on electrical projects. Though he was later forced out due to disagreements with Edison about alternating versus direct current flow, Tesla's system eventually won out. He had invented the most important component of our modern electrical systems—the alternating-current induction motor—by age thirty-two.

His contribution to the use of AC marked the peak of Tesla's monetary success. A visionary to his core, he preferred conceptual design work and allowed his eccentricity to interfere with the business side of inventing. A germophobe and terrible with money, he had visions, believed he'd communicated with aliens, fell in love with a pigeon, and reportedly once relieved Mark Twain of a bout of constipation using his high-frequency oscillator "earthquake machine."

Though he held no patents, he is said to have invented radio, created a remote-controlled boat, fluorescent and neon lights, and an engine turbine that was twenty times more fuel efficient than the piston engine we use today. He also worked tirelessly on the wireless transmission of electricity.

"It seems that I have always been ahead of my time," Tesla said about being forced to wait for the public's interest to catch up to his work. In 2014, more than a century after he conceived of it, scientists at an energy startup powered a house with wireless electricity for the first time. One day, they say, it will be as common as Wi-Fi.

ERNEST HAMWI (SYRIA) Legend has it that Hamwi was selling Syrian waffles, known as *zalabia*, beside ice cream vendor Arnold Fornachou at the 1904 World's Fair in St. Louis. When Fornachou ran out of cups in which to serve ice cream, Hamwi provided folded waffles instead.

JAN ERNST MATZELIGER (BORN IN DUTCH GUIANA, NOW SURINAME) Shoemaking lore says this struggling immigrant salvaged materials from junkyards in the 1880s to create the first shoe-lasting machine, automating the difficult process of joining the shoe leather to its sole, and making shoes affordable for many.

GIDEON SUNDBACK (SWEDEN) An electrical engineer by trade, he was hired to work at Universal Fastener, where in 1913 he moved fastening technology from the time-consuming hook-and-eye strip to the zipper we use today.

JOZEF MURGAŠ (SLOVAKIA) A priest by training, he took an interest in the newly invented telegraph. In his Pennsylvania church basement workshop, he expanded on the design, using musical tones to carry larger volumes of information wirelessly. The innovation would eventually allow for the transmission of the human voice.

PEDRO FLORES (PHILIPPINES) While working odd jobs around Santa Barbara, California, in the 1920s, he saw an opportunity to bring the traditional Filipino bandalore toy to the American market. While his wasn't the first patent for a yo-yo in the States, he changed the knot inside the mechanism to a loop that allowed the user to do tricks, like put the yo-yo to "sleep."

EDWARD BOK (NETHERLANDS) The editor of *Ladies' Home Journal* at the turn of the twentieth century, he coined the term *living room* to describe what had previously been known as a drawing room or parlor. With the change, he encouraged people to use all the rooms and furniture in their houses, rather than setting aside some just for special occasions.

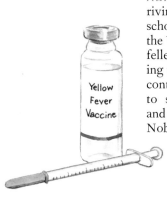

MAX THEILER (SOUTH AFRICA) Arriving in the States after medical school, he became the director of the Virus Laboratory at the Rockefeller Foundation. While developing the vaccine for yellow fever, he contracted the virus, but survived to see the project's completion and become the first African-born Nobel laureate.

LUTHER GEORGE SIMJIAN (ETHNICALLY ARMENIAN, BORN IN OTTOMAN EMPIRE, NOW TURKEY) Separated from his family during the Armenian genocide, he moved to New York City in the 1930s. There he combined technology and banking to create the automated teller machine (ATM). He sold the concept to City Bank of New York for a six-month trial, but it was discontinued due to lack of use by patrons.

SHIRAZ SHIVJI (TANZANIA) After coming to the United States to study electrical engineering, he helped develop the 1982 Commodore 64, an early desktop computer, and later became the head designer for the Atari 520ST and Atari TT computers.

HEDY LAMARR (AUSTRIA) Though most know her as a bombshell actress and the first to depict a female orgasm on film, in her off-hours she was engrossed in a different kind of explosion. In the 1940s she invented and patented a secure radio frequency–hopping system, later used by the military to control torpedoes remotely; the technology became the basis for today's GPS, Wi-Fi, and Bluetooth.

ALEXEY PAJITNOV (RUSSIA) Anyone who's spent hours transfixed before a 1990s computer or Game Boy almost certainly has Pajitnov to thank: His video game Tetris was the first entertainment software to be exported from the Soviet Union to the United States. He later moved to the States to work on the Microsoft Entertainment Pack.

ELON MUSK (SOUTH AFRICA) Founder of the company SpaceX and co-founder of Tesla Inc.; his current plans include a high-speed public transportation Hyperloop, self-driving cars, and a colony to sustain human life on Mars.

LOUISE LITTLE

Migrated from Grenada in 1920

Many have tried to erase her.

History texts, if they name her at all, mention Louise Little as the bearer of seven children, a competent wife to black activist Earl Little, and mother to Malcolm Little, who would emerge from prison as Malcolm X.

In her most famous son's autobiography, Malcolm wrote of his mother's "white" features—the result of her own mother's rape by an older white man, and the reason behind Malcolm's light skin. He described her picky eating habits, and cast her experience of institutionalization as an example of the way government uses faux concern about people's well-being to control black families. But across the breadth of the text, she was little more than a footnote.

In life, too, hate groups and government officials alike tried repeatedly to be rid of her. She and her family were run out of Omaha, then Milwaukee. After the suspicious death of her husband, whom she believed was murdered by a white-supremacist group, she was confined by the state to a Kalamazoo, Michigan, mental hospital for more than twenty years, her children placed in foster care.

But almost no one speaks of her fluency in three languages or of her stubborn self-sufficiency as a female landholder in America's heartland. Few know of her work as a secretary for the Universal Negro Improvement Association (UNIA) and her grassroots activism for Marcus Garvey and other leaders of the Pan-African movement, of her steady insistence that her light-skinned children resist colorism, and that they read the UNIA newsletter *Negro World* and study Grenadian newspapers. Neither her son nor the rest of us seem able to admit what's clear: Without Louise there would be no Malcolm, and without her work centering black pride and Pan-Africanism as foundational pillars of her family, there would be no Malcolm X.

FAZLUR RAHMAN KHAN

Migrated from Bangladesh in 1952

★

When Fazlur Khan arrived at the University of Illinois as a Fulbright scholar, the Empire State Building had been the tallest skyscraper in the world for decades. But it was an inefficient design, requiring massive steel structures through its core to keep standing. Khan, who excelled in mathematics and the humanities, often spoke of the importance of mixing the two to optimize one's critical thinking and problem-solving skills. His passion for both numbers and poetry allowed him to create a new, less-is-more approach to design. He'd come to call it "elegant simplicity."

The result was one of the biggest advances in modern-day architecture: Khan's idea for tube frame construction. The method uses rows of vertical tubing in a building's exterior frame to carry the brunt of the building's load. It requires less steel, leaves more space in the interior, allows for building shapes beyond traditional squares and rectangles, and distributes weight more evenly, offering protection against earthquakes and high winds.

Khan's designs for Chicago's Plaza on DeWitt and the John Hancock Center were the first to test the tube frame. He went on to design the Sears Tower, which reigned as the world's tallest building from 1974 to 1996. Tube frames are still used in all the buildings that have since surpassed the Sears Tower in height.

As an architect and professor, Khan continued to champion the humanities as an inspiration for elegant simplicity, encouraging designers not to allow technology to overtake them but to pursue balance. "The technical man must not be lost in his own technology," he told the *Engineering News-Record* shortly before being named the magazine's Construction's Man of the Year in 1972. "He must be able to appreciate life, and life is art, drama, music, and, most importantly, people."

CÉSAR PELLI (ARGENTINA) World Financial Center, a campus of six shopping centers and office-space buildings in Battery Park, New York City.

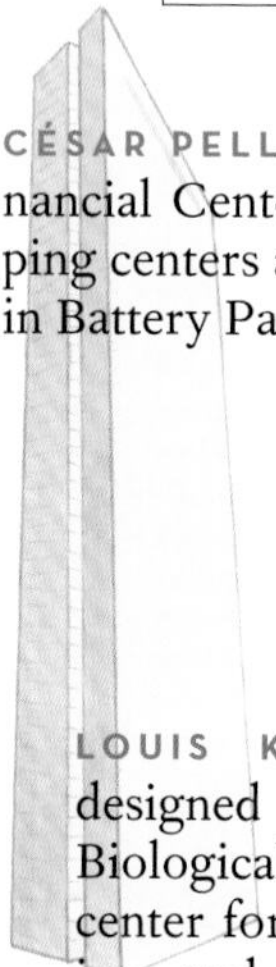

I. M. PEI (CHINA) His celebrated firm is responsible for the John Hancock Tower in Boston, Massachusetts, a sixty-story skyscraper and the tallest building in New England.

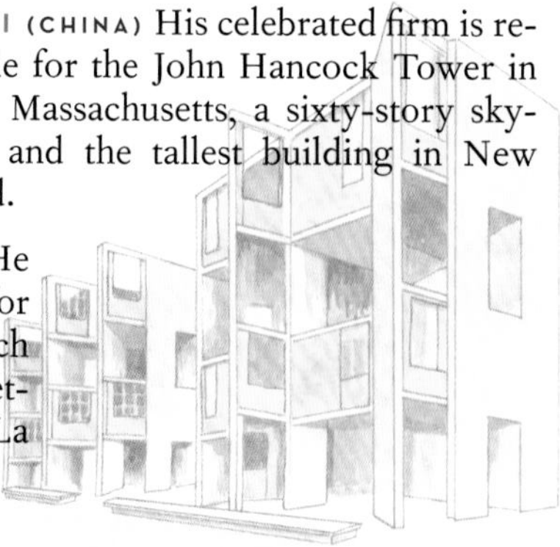

LOUIS KAHN (ESTONIA) He designed the Salk Institute for Biological Studies, a research center for neuroscience, genetics, and immunology in La Jolla, California.

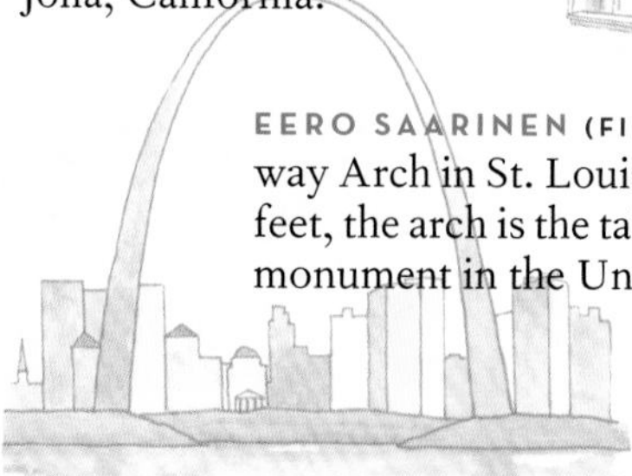

EERO SAARINEN (FINLAND) The Gateway Arch in St. Louis, Missouri; at 630 feet, the arch is the tallest human-made monument in the United States.

JOHN LATENSER (LIECHTENSTEIN) At one time, nearly 91 percent of all blocks in Omaha, Nebraska's downtown district contained one or more buildings designed by John Latenser and Sons. More than a dozen of them are on the National Registry of Historic Places today. Pictured here, the Omaha Athletic Club.

OLGIVANNA LLOYD WRIGHT (MONTENEGRO) A dancer and theosophist, she influenced her husband's design aesthetic and worked tirelessly to keep his legacy alive after his death. Pictured here at Taliesin West, home of his foundation and the School of Architecture in Scottsdale, Arizona.

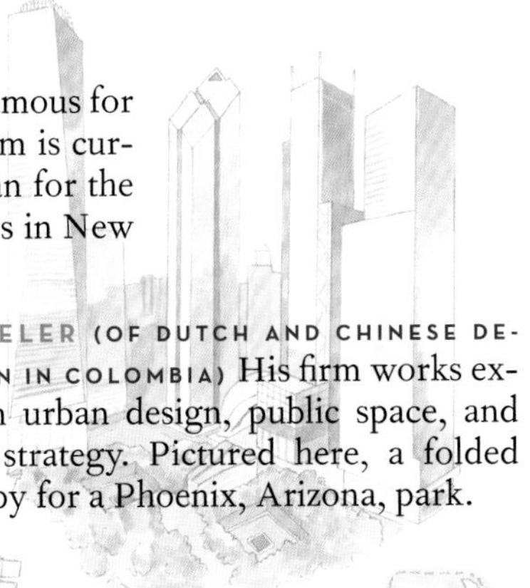

DANIEL LIBESKIND (POLAND) Famous for several museum buildings, his firm is currently in charge of the master plan for the new World Trade Center grounds in New York City.

ERIC HÖWELER (OF DUTCH AND CHINESE DESCENT, BORN IN COLOMBIA) His firm works extensively in urban design, public space, and immersive strategy. Pictured here, a folded metal canopy for a Phoenix, Arizona, park.

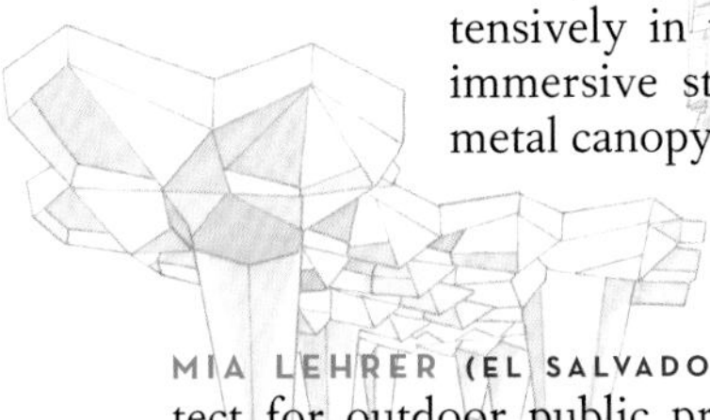

MIA LEHRER (EL SALVADOR) Landscape architect for outdoor public projects in California, she planned the gardens at the Natural History Museum of Los Angeles County, the San Pedro waterfront revitalization, and the Silver Lake Reservoir, pictured here.

TEDDY CRUZ (GUATEMALA) A professor at the University of California, San Diego, he examines how urban design can be used to support civic engagement. One of his proposals includes merging spaces for senior housing and childcare, community-centered design he calls "bottom-up architecture." His projects are often located in marginalized neighborhoods of San Diego.

IVAN MEŠTROVIĆ

Migrated from Austria-Hungary
(now Croatia) in 1947

Rodin once called him "the greatest phenomenon amongst sculptors." The president of the University of Notre Dame declared him "the Michelangelo of his time." When Ivan Meštrović had an exhibition at the Metropolitan Museum of Art, the editor of *Arts Magazine* reviewed it, hailing him as "almost unanimously revered by American sculptors of all schools as one of the greatest living sculptors."

But today, nearly fifty years after his death, few people know Meštrović's name. Many are unwittingly familiar with his works, though—large sculptures in stone, bronze, and wood that are displayed in museums and public forums around the world.

Born in the Croatian countryside and raised in the Dinaric Alps, Meštrović was the child of peasant shepherds and had little formal education. At sixteen, he became apprenticed to a stonemason, where his talent was recognized almost immediately, but after his arrest by a contingent of Croatian fascist sympathizers, he immigrated to the United States. Meštrović rose quickly to stardom in the American scene, receiving commissions, exhibitions, and professorships around the country, and was extremely prolific, crafting hundreds of sculptures during his years in the States.

His obscurity today is perhaps by his own design. Stricken with grief over the death of two of his children, Meštrović spent his last days making four clay sculptures in memorial to them, then died shortly thereafter. Still, without knowing his name, hundreds of thousands of Americans continue to pass by his work each day: Two large bronzes, *The Bowman* and *The Spearman*, stand guard over Chicago's Congress Plaza, and *St. Jerome the Priest* sits reading on Embassy Row in Washington, D.C.

LAURENT CLERC

Migrated from France in 1816

★

His destiny was forged by fire. As a baby, Laurent Clerc fell from his high chair into the kitchen fireplace, an accident said to have caused his deafness. In sign language, his name is his scar—two fingers brushed across the signer's cheek, where Clerc's flesh was knotted and pale from the burns.

Clerc was a student then a teacher at the Institut National des Jeune Sourds-Muets in Paris, the first deaf school in the world. The institute was a linguistic haven for deaf children, who, rather than focusing their energy on learning speech, studied the academic subjects through French Sign Language (LSF).

Meanwhile, in the United States, there was no standardized sign language, and most deaf people were isolated in rural areas. An American, Reverend Thomas Gallaudet, traveled to Europe seeking a method of education for deaf children.

In Paris he met Clerc, by then a respected teacher and public rhetorician. Clerc wrote books, gave lectures, and knew several languages. He was adored by students and colleagues for his sardonic wit—while his signed name is placed in reference to his scar, LSF also makes use of the same handshape and movement as part of the sign for *funny*. When Gallaudet saw him give a lecture, he asked Clerc to come to the States to help organize the first deaf school in North America.

In 1817, Clerc and Gallaudet founded the American School for the Deaf in Hartford, Connecticut, where Clerc would teach for the next forty-one years. Clerc's French Sign Language, melded with other signs carried by students from across the country, became the American Sign Language used today.

DIANE VON FURSTENBERG

Migrated from Belgium via France in 1970

★

"I never knew what I wanted to do. But I knew the kind of woman I wanted to be," Diane von Furstenberg said in a recent interview with *Makers.* "I wanted to be an independent woman, a woman who could pay for her bills, a woman who can run her own life."

It was a goal she'd achieve many times over. As a fashion designer and icon, wife, mother, and—for a time, while wed to Prince Egon von Fürstenberg—a princess, Furstenberg is living proof that women can have it all.

She learned fearlessness from her mother, an Auschwitz survivor. In her, Furstenberg saw a model of strength and femininity intertwined, a combination she would later wield to revolutionize the fashion industry with her idea for the wrap dress.

"I was always a little bit of a feminist," said Furstenberg. "Doesn't mean that if you're a feminist you have to look like a truck driver." At a time when women had taken to structured clothes as masculine-inspired symbols of strength, Furstenberg designed soft wrap dresses in bold prints that were affordable, flattering for a variety of body types, and functional for the modern woman. A wrap dress tightly belted was a perfect fit for women at the office, and the belt could be loosened to lower the neckline after hours, allowing for a seamless transition into every part of life.

Recently, Furstenberg has taken to philanthropy as a means of supporting female empowerment, serving on the board of Vital Voices, an organization that fosters entrepreneurship globally among women. She's also a board member for the Statue of Liberty–Ellis Island Foundation, dedicated to the care and keeping of the island as a beacon of America's immigrant tradition.

Many of the snacks, style choices, vehicles, and even toys we consider iconically "American" wouldn't be here without their immigrant inventors. How many can you spot throughout your week?

LEVI STRAUSS
(GERMANY)
Levi's jeans

LOUIS LASSEN
(DENMARK)
Hamburgers

CARL SWANSON
(SWEDEN) Swanson chicken broth and frozen foods

LOUIS CHEVROLET
(SWITZERLAND)
Chevy cars and trucks

NATHAN HANDWERKER (POLAND)
Nathan's Famous hot dogs

ETTORE BOIARDI (ITALY)
Chef Boyardee

TOM CARVEL (GREECE)
Carvel ice cream and cakes

NASSER WEDDADY

Migrated from Mauritania in 1999

★

The revolution was televised. More important, the revolution was on Twitter. From Nasser Weddady's office on Newbury Street—an affluent Boston district known for its designer shops—a new kind of activism was born. Thousands of miles away from the action, Weddady was one of a decentralized core group of leaders in the series of revolutions that came to be known as the Arab Spring.

Running on lattes and cigarettes, Weddady coordinated with other activists globally to organize protests and campaign—often successfully—for the release of detained protesters and journalists. He crafted easily digestible analyses of the complicated political contexts of the uprising for American journalists and news networks to quote, and used his understanding of the twenty-four-hour news cycle to time the release of information for maximum impact.

Some of Weddady's cyberactivist counterparts didn't speak Arabic and had never been to the Middle East. The son of a diplomat, Weddady himself had lived in Libya, Benin, Syria, Ethiopia, and Nigeria, and is fluent in Arabic, French, Spanish, Hebrew, and English. His activism hadn't always been at a distance; as a teenager in his home country of Mauritania, he was part of a radical movement that opposed government crackdowns on political and religious organizations it deemed a threat. Fearing retribution, he fled, leaving his family behind.

While few on the streets of Boston would give him a second look, fellow activists speak of him admiringly, describing him as "omnipresent." He has more than forty thousand Twitter followers.

Does he ever take a break from tweeting the revolution? "Sometimes," he told *The Atlantic*, "I'm on planes."

PEGGIELENE BARTELS

Migrated from Ghana in the 1970s

When Peggielene Bartels was roused by an early-morning phone call from her cousin telling her that she had been chosen as her people's next ruler, she thought it was a prank and nearly hung up on him. Bartels had been a U.S. citizen for more than a decade and was leading an unassuming life in a one-bedroom apartment outside Washington, D.C. It seemed impossible that thousands of miles away in her hometown of Otuam, a fishing village in Ghana, a series of rituals had anointed her as her late uncle's successor.

But the four A.M. call to duty was no joke, and after some deliberation, Bartels accepted, provided she could maintain a version of the life she'd built in the States. As she was the first female leader of Otuam, there was no precedent on what she might be called. Not liking the sound of "queen," she decided she would be "king" just as the men before her had been; the people of Otuam refer to her as "King Peggy," or sometimes "Nana."

In America, she drives, cooks, cleans, and holds down the same job she's had since the 1970s—administrative assistant in Ghana's embassy in Washington, D.C. Back in Otuam, she wears a crown, and people try to serve and bow to her, which sometimes bothers her. "I want them to be free and comfortable," she told CNN, "so that way we can really address issues."

Bartels calls Otuam at one o'clock each morning to check in with her regent and royal council, and uses her vacation time to spend a month there each year. Her reign so far has brought a better quality of life for her people, providing school fees, computers, a town ambulance, and clean drinking water.

Often revolutionaries in their native countries, these leaders in exile made a home for themselves in the United States, though the distance rarely stopped them from continuing their work.

JOSÉ ANTONIO PÁEZ (VENEZUELA) A crusader for Venezuelan independence—first from the Spanish crown, then as a nation separate from Gran Colombia—Páez served twice as president, helping establish the new nation before his exile to New York City.

DILUWA KHUTUGTU JAMSRANGJAB (MONGO-LIA) Believed by his followers to be an incarnation of Buddha, he fled to the United States due to political persecution and became a scholar and professor at Johns Hopkins University. While in the United States, he continued to fight for the recognition of Mongolian independence by the United Nations.

EDUARDO MONDLANE (MOZAMBIQUE) A student at Oberlin College and then a professor at Syracuse University, he founded the Mozambique Liberation Front, which fought to secure the country's independence from Portugal. He was assassinated in 1969.

KIGELI V (RWANDA) The last ruling king of Rwanda before the monarchy was abolished, he spent much of his life in exile. Making a humble life for himself in Virginia, he ran a humanitarian foundation for Rwandan refugees in the wake of the genocide there.

LOBSANG SANGAY (TIBET) Born a refugee in India, he's currently the ruler of Tibet's government-in-exile. He arrived in the United States as a Fulbright scholar attending Harvard Law School, and is now a U.S. citizen and Boston resident. The first democratically elected person and non-monk to head the Tibetan government, this globally minded academic has energized young Tibetan activists to continue the fight for independence.

SAINT RAPHAEL

SAINT RAPHAEL OF BROOKLYN

Migrated from Syria in 1895

★

Brooklyn, New York, has only one saint—a nineteenth-century Syrian refugee turned Orthodox priest named Raphael Hawaweeny. Hawaweeny's life was centered on the church from his first moments—he was born in Beirut while his family was fleeing the massacre of Christians in Damascus. When they returned to Syria, Hawaweeny showed promise as a student, but his family couldn't afford to pay for school. A deacon interceded, redirecting Hawaweeny's education to prepare him for priesthood.

He studied Orthodox Christianity in Greece, Russia, and Syria. After his ordination, he set his sights on the Orthodox congregants of America, particularly in the Syrian community. Often made up of small pockets of migrants who lived far away from the nearest Orthodox church, many Orthodox Christian communities in America struggled to keep the faith without resources. Hawaweeny dedicated the rest of his life to serving those believers.

He traveled across North America performing the priestly duties of baptism, marriage, and burial for Orthodox communities. He wrote an Arabic prayer-and-liturgy book that was adopted by congregations everywhere, and founded *The Word* magazine, the official publication of the Antiochian Archdiocese. Originally in Arabic, the magazine switched to English in 1957, and is still published today.

All the while, Hawaweeny tended to his congregants in New York City foremost, founding his first parish in Brooklyn. He established a total of thirty Orthodox parishes across America in his lifetime, and in 1904 was the first Orthodox bishop to be consecrated on U.S. soil.

Hawaweeny was canonized by the church as Saint Raphael in 2000. A relic of his finger bone remains on display in Saint Nicholas Antiochian Orthodox Cathedral in Brooklyn.

MELANIA TRUMP

Migrated from Slovenia (formerly Yugoslavia)
in 1996

The only naturalized citizen ever to become First Lady, Melania Trump grew up Melanija Knavs in the small Yugoslavian town of Sevnica. Aligned with neither the United States nor the Soviet Union in the Cold War era, Yugoslavia had an overarching Communist government but permitted certain individual freedoms, which allowed for humble but comfortable middle-class existences like that of Knavs's family.

Knavs, her parents, and her younger sister lived in a standard concrete-block apartment; according to school friends she was a good student who excelled in geography. She liked to read and knit. She is remembered by many in her hometown as beautiful, but perhaps the only detail of her childhood that might foreshadow her future pursuits was her mother's involvement in the clothing industry—she's sometimes described as a textile factory worker or a designer of children's clothing.

By sixteen, Knavs had entered the fashion world of her own accord as a commercial model named Melania Knauss, working in Paris and Milan before migrating to the United States. Once in New York City, she also established her own jewelry and skincare lines.

Today, Melania Trump seems firmly rooted in the States, her diminishing accent and fluency in five languages the only hint of her foreign past.

Her family still owns a house in Sevnica (now Slovenia), but Trump visits rarely, with her husband reportedly having been in the country only once, for a few hours, to dine with her parents. But while her interest in Slovenia might appear to have faded, Melania did think of home after the birth of her son, Barron: She donated $25,000 to Sevnica's clinic to improve maternity and neonatal care.

DANIELLE BAHI (IVORY COAST) She founded Bahi Cosmetics, an organic, vegan, and cruelty-free cosmetics company for women of every color, in her dorm room at age nineteen.

DO WON AND JIN SOOK CHANG (SOUTH KOREA) This husband-and-wife team founded the multibillion-dollar international clothing chain Forever 21.

TARIQ FARID (PAKISTAN) Working in the family floral shop in Connecticut, he developed software specifically for floral businesses, eventually founding Edible Arrangements, a gift company that crosses fruit baskets with floral arrangements to deliver fresh-fruit bouquets.

CLAUDE GRUNITZKY (TOGO) A graduate of London University and MIT, he used his business acumen to found *TRACE* magazine and TV network, spotlighting urban and international popular culture trends and icons.

SIR W. ARTHUR LEWIS (BORN IN ST. LUCIA TO ANTIGUAN PARENTS) Knighted in 1963 and awarded the 1979 Nobel Prize for his work, he invented the dual-sector, or "Lewis" model, which examines the transition of labor between capitalist and subsistence sectors of a developing economy.

RUPERT MURDOCH (AUSTRALIA) He got his start purchasing newspapers across Australia and New Zealand, the United Kingdom, and the United States, eventually forming News Corporation. He's since served as CEO of News Corporation, 21st Century Fox, and Fox News Channel, with a current net worth of $18.9 billion.

DAVID NEELEMAN (BRAZIL) He founded JetBlue, WestJet, Morris Air, and Azul Brazilian Airlines, and is the co-owner of TAP Air Portugal; his current plan is for a new, low-cost U.S. airline that will travel only between secondary airports.

INDRA NOOYI (INDIA) CEO of PepsiCo for twelve years, she is consistently ranked as one of the world's one hundred most powerful women by *Forbes*.

GEORGE SOROS (HUNGARY) A survivor of the Nazi occupation of Hungary, he became a successful hedge fund manager and renowned philanthropist. His current net worth is about $8 billion after having donated more than $32 billion to Open Society Foundations, his grantmaking agency, which supports human rights protections, education, and public health initiatives.

HAMDI ULUKAYA (TURKEY) Born into a small-town dairy-farming family in Turkey, he's now the billionaire founder and CEO of the United States' leading Greek yogurt company, Chobani. He builds his plants in economically struggling U.S. regions, offers job training and living wages for his manufacturing employees, and frequently donates to organizations that support refugees.

CREATORS

JONI MITCHELL

Migrated from Canada in 1965

★

She took piano lessons as a child and taught herself to play the ukulele and the guitar as a teen, but at first music was just for fun. Then it became a means to pursue her true passions: painting and smoking—a habit she picked up at age nine in her rural hometown of Saskatoon. "Music was firstly a hobby to make money to smoke at art school," Joni Mitchell told *The Telegraph* in 2007. She took on gigs at nightclubs, coffee houses, and local radio shows to earn money, but eventually dropped out of Alberta College of Art, disillusioned by its emphasis on technical skill rather than originality. In 1965 she moved to the States to explore the folk music scene.

Over the next several decades, Mitchell would find fame in both folk and mainstream music. *Rolling Stone* would hail her "one of the greatest songwriters ever," while AllMusic made a case for her as "the most important and influential female recording artist of the 21st century." She's won nine Grammys, including a Lifetime Achievement Award, and was featured on a Canadian postage stamp. With each album, she prioritized the originality she craved from her art school days, experimenting with sounds borrowed from pop, jazz, classical, and world music. She composed songs on the guitar in more than fifty different tunings, using invented configurations she called "Joni's weird chords."

"I thrive on change," she said of both her chords and her lifestyle. "That's probably why my chord changes are weird, because chords depict emotions. They'll be going along on one key and I'll drop off a cliff, and suddenly they will go into a whole other key signature. That will drive some people crazy, but that's how my life is."

WILLEM DE KOONING

Migrated from the Netherlands in 1926

Willem de Kooning had tried to stow away before. Long interested in American pop culture, he had hidden on ships in an attempt to make it to the United States but was always caught, or found himself on a docked boat going nowhere. But in 1926, an acquaintance set to work as a waiter on the Virginia-bound SS *Shelley* told him he could hide in the engine room if he didn't bring much with him. Without telling his family, and without his art portfolio, de Kooning boarded the ship.

In America, de Kooning made ends meet as a painter, but not the kind he aspired to be—he took on carpentry work and painted houses. He'd later incorporate the large brushes he used for those jobs into his artwork. In 1935, he was hired by the WPA Federal Art Project, but left due to fears that his undocumented status would be discovered. Now fully immersed in the New York art scene, de Kooning was influenced by the Jazz Age; his studio-mate, Arshile Gorky; and the work of foundational cubists, surrealists, and "action painters" in developing his own abstract expressionist style.

For de Kooning, abstraction and representation weren't mutually exclusive. Of his artistic process he said: "I'm not interested in 'abstracting' or taking things out or reducing painting to design, form, line, and color. I paint this way because I can keep putting more things in it—drama, anger, pain, love, a figure, a horse, my ideas about space. Through your eyes it again becomes an emotion or idea."

While he achieved mainstream success in his lifetime and was considered a leader by his peers, de Kooning himself had his eye on the success and ingenuity of his contemporary Pablo Picasso, whom he once called "the man to beat."

KHALED HOSSEINI

Migrated from Afghanistan in 1980

★

Before his acclaimed novel *The Kite Runner* spent over two years as a number one *New York Times* bestseller, was translated into forty-two languages, and sold more than thirty-eight million copies worldwide, it was a discarded short story in Khaled Hosseini's garage.

Hosseini had arrived in the United States as a freshman in high school and spoke no English. His father and mother, a diplomat and a high school vice principal in Afghanistan, now struggled to make ends meet. Hosseini poured himself into his studies, pledging to provide financial stability for the family by becoming a doctor.

He made good on the promise but found medicine unfulfilling, comparing the work to an arranged marriage. He'd find his real passion buried in a 1999 news report about the rise of the Taliban, and their penchant for declaring nearly all hobbies "un-Islamic." It was their ban on kite flying that stuck in the craw of Hosseini's imagination as a particular cruelty: He had fond memories of flying kites with his cousins in Kabul. He wrote a short story about two boys who flew kites together and submitted it to a few big magazines, but it was rejected.

Hosseini continued working as a physician, but when he uncovered the story years later, he found its hold on him had not lessened. He began to expand on the lives of the two boys until they grew into the novel that would propel him to literary stardom.

Despite his success, Hosseini speaks of *The Kite Runner* like most writers do of their debuts, telling *The Guardian*, "If I were given a red pen now . . . I'd take that thing apart."

RECOMMENDED READING:
GREAT AMERICAN NOVELS

*I would give most anything to hear my father's
talk again, the crash and bang and stop of
his language, always hurtling by. I will listen for
him forever in the streets of this city.*

—CHANG-RAE LEE *Native Speaker*

HENRY ROTH **(AUSTRIA-HUNGARY, NOW UKRAINE)**
Call It Sleep, 1934

AYN RAND **(RUSSIA)** *The Fountainhead,* 1943

VLADIMIR NABOKOV **(RUSSIA)** *Pale Fire,* 1962

ISAAC ASIMOV **(RUSSIA)** *The Gods Themselves,* 1972

ROSEMARY ROGERS **(CEYLON, NOW SRI LANKA)**
Sweet Savage Love, 1974

EDWIDGE DANTICAT **(HAITI)**
Breath, Eyes, Memory, 1994

CHANG-RAE LEE (SOUTH KOREA) *Native Speaker*, 1995

COLUM McCANN (IRELAND)
Let the Great World Spin, 2009

ABRAHAM VERGHESE (ETHIOPIA) *Cutting for Stone*, 2009

TÉA OBREHT (YUGOSLAVIA, NOW BOSNIA,
SLOVENIA, AND SERBIA) *The Tiger's Wife*, 2010

CHIMAMANDA NGOZI ADICHIE (NIGERIA)
Americanah, 2013

NOVIOLET BULAWAYO (ZIMBABWE)
We Need New Names, 2013

KEVIN KWAN (SINGAPORE) *Crazy Rich Asians*, 2013

VIET THANH NGUYEN (VIETNAM) *The Sympathizer*, 2015

YAA GYASI (GHANA) *Homegoing*, 2016

IMBOLO MBUE (CAMEROON) *Behold the Dreamers*, 2016

NAMWALI SERPELL (ZAMBIA) *The Old Drift*, 2019

FLEA

Migrated from Australia circa 1966

Michael Peter Balzary, more commonly known as the Red Hot Chili Peppers' co-founder and bassist Flea, is into another kind of bug these days: honeybees.

Worried about the decline of the honeybee population and the threat to the food supply that a decrease in bee pollination could cause, Flea built an apiary in his backyard, playing keeper for more than two hundred thousand insects, to whom he lovingly refers as "Flea's bees."

It's one of many causes the musician has taken on over the years. His frenzied, fidgety nature makes it easy to see how he earned his nickname: As a child he was called "Mike B the Flea" due to his inability to sit still. Today, Flea's varied philanthropic interests include climate change, gun control, the Silverlake Conservatory of Music, Tibetan independence, Rock the Vote, Hurricane Katrina victims' funds, and the Special Olympics.

Of late, Flea has also been speaking out about the United States' opioid crisis. Rarely one to reveal personal struggles, Flea penned an op-ed for *Time* chronicling a childhood scarred by abuse and addiction, describing himself as a "petty thievin' Hollywood street urchin running feral, and doing every drug in the book."

He's come a long way from urchin to Flea: *Rolling Stone* named him the second-greatest bassist of all time, behind the Who's John Entwistle, and he and the rest of the Chili Peppers were inducted into the Rock and Roll Hall of Fame in 2012.

In addition to playing on the Chili Peppers' twentieth album, which is expected in 2019, Flea continues to surprise outside the world of rock and roll: He plays the trumpet, runs marathons, and has acted in dozens of movies and television shows, including providing the voice of another young feral boy, Donnie, from Nickelodeon's *The Wild Thornberrys*.

CAROLINA HERRERA

Migrated from Venezuela in 1980

★

Carolina Herrera—lifelong socialite, International Best-Dressed Hall of Famer, designer for first ladies—is painfully shy.

Herrera grew up in luxury, the daughter of a former governor of Caracas, with fond childhood memories of being gussied up in designer dresses, attending fashion shows with her grandmother, and sewing clothes for her dolls.

When she moved to New York City as an adult, she slid easily into the city's socialite scene. She was a regular at Studio 54, and was considered one of Andy Warhol's muses.

Though Herrera landed frequently on best-dressed lists and had designed clothes for herself and her friends, she hadn't considered a profession in fashion. She was working as a publicist when her friend and former editor in chief of *Vogue*, Diana Vreeland, suggested she create a collection. In 1981, at the age of forty-one, Herrera made her designing debut at the Metropolitan Club; the budding supermodel Iman walked in the show.

Though some had initially scoffed at the idea of such a late entry into the design world, Herrera was a quick success. She became known for dressing duchesses, princesses, and America's First Ladies, including Jacqueline Kennedy Onassis, Laura Bush, and Michelle Obama.

But her quiet nature never left her, and Herrera still prefers to let her clothes speak for themselves. "When I go to a charity ball, I don't mind if people look at my sleeves," she said in an interview with *People*.

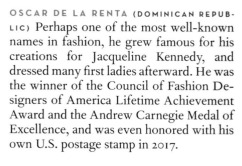

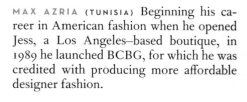

OSCAR DE LA RENTA (DOMINICAN REPUB-LIC) Perhaps one of the most well-known names in fashion, he grew famous for his creations for Jacqueline Kennedy, and dressed many first ladies afterward. He was the winner of the Council of Fashion Designers of America Lifetime Achievement Award and the Andrew Carnegie Medal of Excellence, and was even honored with his own U.S. postage stamp in 2017.

IWAN TIRTA (INDONESIA) Credited with reviving a traditional Indonesian wax-dyeing method called batik, he designed handmade clothes for the Reagans and Nelson Mandela.

MAX AZRIA (TUNISIA) Beginning his career in American fashion when he opened Jess, a Los Angeles–based boutique, in 1989 he launched BCBG, for which he was credited with producing more affordable designer fashion.

CHLOE DAO (VIETNAM) Born in Laos to refugees of the Vietnam War, she won season two of the television competition *Project Runway;* she continues to design her own clothing line and runs a Houston-based boutique.

THAKOON PANICHGUL (THAILAND) He started off as a fashion writer in Omaha, where he was raised; his versatile, feminine designs appeal to haute couture–wearing movie stars and shoppers of his Gap and Target collections alike.

PRABAL GURUNG (NEPAL) Using fashion as a means of activism, he prioritizes U.S.-based production and donated a portion of his recent T-shirt collection proceeds to Planned Parenthood, the ACLU, and Shikshya Foundation Nepal. He's dressed Michelle Obama, the Duchess of Cambridge, and many other celebrities.

HÉLÈNE ARPELS (MONACO) Born in Monte Carlo to parents of Russian descent, she was a luxury shoe designer whose heels were a well-known favorite of Jacqueline Kennedy.

PATRICIA VELÁSQUEZ (VENEZUELA) A runway and print model for high-fashion designers like Chanel and Dolce & Gabbana, she's considered by many to be the first Latina supermodel, the first indigenous supermodel, and one of the first supermodels to be openly gay.

GRACE JONES (JAMAICA) First famous as a supermodel whose androgynous looks were a hit in both the Paris and New York fashion scenes, she later transitioned seamlessly into the music and film industries. "Everyone from Madonna to Björk to Beyoncé to Lady Gaga has taken more than a few pages from her playbook," *W* magazine said of the star.

ANNA WINTOUR (UNITED KINGDOM) The editor in chief of *Vogue* and artistic director of Condé Nast, she is believed to be the inspiration for the iconic Miranda Priestly character in the bestseller *The Devil Wears Prada*, played by Meryl Streep in the movie adaptation.

GISELE BÜNDCHEN (BRAZIL). Sometimes called Brazil's most famous export, she was one of the first Brazilian models to find international success, and shifted the industry paradigm back toward sexy, curvier models and away from the ultra-thin aesthetic that prevailed in the 1990s. She remains among the highest paid models in the world.

ARMANDO CABRAL (GUINEA-BISSAU/PORTUGAL) Globetrotting as a model and designer for some of the fashion world's biggest houses, he eventually struck out on his own to create a brand of men's luxury shoes that are comfortable enough to stand up to everyday travels.

JENNY BUI

Migrated from Cambodia in the 1990s

The Queen of Bling—known for her Swarovski-studded nail designs made famous by rapper Cardi B and adored by more than half a million of her own Instagram followers—had a far-from-glamorous start. The Khmer Rouge came to power in Cambodia when Bui was five, beginning an oppressive rule that included the systematic murder of one to three million ethnic and religious minorities. Bui's family nearly starved; at times they had only papaya bark scrapings to eat.

They fled to a camp in Thailand where they stayed until the Thai government tired of them, leading the refugees up a land mine–riddled mountain with the promise of locating lost family members, then abandoning them there. Bui and her family were forced to make a three-month return journey to Cambodia on foot before eventually escaping to Vietnam, then Canada, when she was fourteen.

She moved to the Bronx when she was twenty-two and learned to do nails by hanging around a friend's salon and testing new ideas on herself until she bled.

When Cardi B first came into the salon, Bui was fond of her right away, though Cardi was still an exotic dancer and couldn't always pay. A few years later, Cardi's music career would rocket them both to stardom.

These days, the world marvels at Bui's sometimes outlandish but always luminescent designs, but she remains Cardi's personal nail stylist. "Our relationship is like I treat her like she's my daughter and she treats me like I'm her aunty," Bui said in an interview with *Cools* magazine. "I'm so happy for her, every time I see her dressed so pretty I never can believe that's my Cardi B."

ISABEL ALLENDE

Migrated from Chile via Venezuela in 1988

★

Isabel Allende was a bad journalist. She had a penchant for making things up. As a reporter, the impulse was a flaw, one that led famed poet Pablo Neruda to call her the "worst journalist in the world" when she met him for what she thought would be an interview. But, according to Allende's memoir, *Paula*, Neruda had more to offer than criticism: He suggested she write fiction, where her "defects" would be "virtues."

It took her almost a decade to heed his advice. Allende fled to Venezuela in 1975, after a CIA-backed coup overthrew her cousin once removed, then–Chilean president Salvador Allende, and installed the dictator Augusto Pinochet. In 1981, still in exile, she learned that her grandfather was on the brink of death. Heartbroken and unable to return, she began writing him a frenzied letter. That letter would become her debut novel, *The House of the Spirits*.

Allende's reception by literary critics is uneven. Some laud her place in the canon and compare her writing to foundational magical realists Jorge Luis Borges and Gabriel García Márquez; others are put off by her commercial success and say her adherence to magical realism as a genre is incomplete.

For her part, Allende sees both sides of her critics' sentiments. Confusing commercial success with one's inability to be a serious writer is, Allende said in a *Guardian* interview, "a great insult to the readership." As for genre, she thinks of her work less as magical realism and more as an attempt to capture the true essence of her family; she's said that her relatives are so strange she does not need to invent much magic.

Of course, magic, like truth, is in the eye of the beholder. "Don't believe everything I say," Allende warns readers on her website. "I tend to exaggerate a bit."

While the astronauts, heroes forever, spent mere hours on the moon, I have remained in this new world for nearly thirty years. I know that my achievement is quite ordinary. I am not the only man to seek his fortune far from home, and certainly I am not the first. Still, there are times I am bewildered by each mile I have traveled, each meal I have eaten, each person I have known, each room in which I have slept. As ordinary as it all appears, there are times when it is beyond my imagination.

—JHUMPA LAHIRI,
"THE THIRD AND FINAL CONTINENT"

ACHY OBEJAS (CUBA)
We Came All the Way from Cuba So
You Could Dress Like This? 1994

JHUMPA LAHIRI (UNITED KINGDOM)
The Interpreter of Maladies, 1999

ALEKSANDAR HEMON (BOSNIA AND HERZEGOVINA)
The Question of Bruno, 2000

ABDOURAHMAN A. WABERI (DJIBOUTI)
The Land Without Shadows, 2005

MIA ALVAR (PHILIPPINES)
In the Country, 2015

JENNY ZHANG (CHINA)
Sour Heart, 2017

CHINUA ACHEBE

Migrated from Nigeria in 1990

★

In the late 1950s, Chinua Achebe sent the only copy of his debut novel, *Things Fall Apart*, to London to seek publication. The manuscript was met with immediate rejection—there was simply no market, they said, for African fiction. When the educational publisher Heinemann eventually decided to take a chance on the book, they printed just two thousand copies.

Things Fall Apart, which chronicles the experience of an Igbo man, Okonkwo, as his life is shattered by the arrival of colonial settlers, is now required reading for high school students everywhere. Having sold more than twenty million copies in fifty-seven languages, Achebe is among the most translated writers in the world.

Achebe's work transformed the concept of the African novel, which before him had mostly meant novels written by white men who'd visited the continent. In and outside of his fiction, he was unafraid to take this model to task, calling the much-lauded writer Joseph Conrad "a bloody racist" and criticizing Nobel Peace Prize laureate Albert Schweitzer for his paternalism. Achebe was also at odds with other African thinkers, notably Kenyan novelist Ngũgĩ wa Thiong'o, over whether a work could be truly "African" if it were written in English. Achebe believed that, for better or worse, English was a tool he'd been given, and one he could use to dismantle colonial power structures.

But for Achebe, language wasn't always a political decision. When *The Paris Review* asked Achebe about his use of the poet Yeats's turn of phrase "Things fall apart" for his title, Achebe said he was an admirer of "that wild Irishman's" work, but that he hadn't been making a statement with its use. "Actually, I wouldn't make too much of that," Achebe said. "I was showing off more than anything else."

Chinua Achebe

ANTHILLS OF THE SAVANNAH

Chinua Achebe

HOME and

Chinua Achebe

Girls at War

HOPES and IMPEDIMENTS

Chinua Achebe

CHIKE and the River

Chinua Achebe

MILA KUNIS

Migrated from Ukraine in 1991

★

She is an unlikely candidate to play the archetypal all-American, Midwestern sweetheart: dark featured with chestnut hair and mismatched eyes—one green, one brown. Her voice is husky, sultry, deep for her small frame. She is Jewish and fled the Ukraine in 1991 seeking refuge from religious persecution.

Mila Kunis was seven when she and her family arrived in Los Angeles with $250 to their name. Her parents were professionals in their home country—a physicist and a mechanical engineer—but their degrees meant little in California.

Kunis knew no English, and cried her way through the second grade. Her parents enrolled her in an acting class as a way to practice the new language, but she quickly became serious about the craft and began to land commercials and minor parts on television shows.

At fourteen she scored an audition for a leading TV role. All the actors were supposed to be over eighteen, but she fudged her age until the producers promised her the job. For the next eight years she was Point Place, Wisconsin, bombshell Jackie Burkhart on *That '70s Show*. The slightly conceited, ever fashionable Jackie was a far cry from the WASPy women and girls who almost exclusively served as leading ladies in late '90s sitcoms, not to mention the 1970s shows after which her show was modeled. The country fell in love with her anyway.

In 2015 she married her TV high-school sweetheart, Ashton Kutcher, who'd played opposite her on the show. She speaks Russian to their two children, Wyatt and Dimitri.

ANGÉLIQUE KIDJO

Migrated from Benin via Paris in the 1980s

★

Throughout her life, people have often tried—and failed—to neatly categorize Angélique Kidjo, her family, and her sound.

She was raised in a musical household: Her mother was a choreographer and theater director, and her father introduced her to an unlikely mix of Fela Kuti, Jimi Hendrix, James Brown, and traditional Beninese music. While others in the community likened musical performance, particularly by young women, to prostitution, her father championed both her music and education, support that led some neighbors to disparage him as a sell-out to white ways of thinking.

Kidjo left Benin for France in 1983 after refusing to write music that exclusively praised her country's then-Communist government. But when she attended jazz school at CIM in Paris, she was told by white students that jazz was not for Africans; she stood out even more once it was clear that she didn't read music.

Even now, after decades of stardom and an award-winning discography, critics have both hailed her as the queen of African music and questioned the authenticity of her work, calling it overproduced and accusing her of not being "African enough," her sound tarnished by the Western influence in her rhythms.

But Kidjo, who is also an activist with UNICEF and Oxfam, eschews the idea of purity as an end goal both musically and politically. "What is pure in nature?" she said in an interview with *Pitchfork*. "The fact that we keep ourselves divided is exactly what the people in power want us to do. The more divided you are, the more power you give them, and the more they can kill you."

Kidjo's three Grammys suggest that refusing to collapse oneself into a single category is the best way to make lasting music after all.

SANTANA AND FRIENDS

CARLOS SANTANA (MEXICO) **is one of American music's most beloved guitarists, known for fusing rock and Latin American jazz rhythms. He's also famous for his collaborations with other musicians, including several other immigrants.**

"GET UPPA" with Jerry Garcia and Steve Jordan

"DO YOU LIKE THE WAY" with Lauryn Hill and CeeLo Green

"THE CALLING" with Eric Clapton

"LOVE OF MY LIFE" with Dave Matthews (SOUTH AFRICA)

"MARIA, MARIA" with The Product G&B

"PUT YOUR LIGHTS ON" with Everlast

"SMOOTH" with Rob Thomas

"WHATEVER HAPPENS" with Michael Jackson

"THE GAME OF LOVE" with Tina Turner and again with Michelle Branch

"ILLEGAL" with Shakira (COLOMBIA)

"JUST FEEL BETTER" with Steven Tyler

"NO LLORES" with Gloria Estefan (CUBA)

"PEARLS" with Angélique Kidjo (BENIN)

"WHILE MY GUITAR GENTLY WEEPS" with Yo-Yo Ma (FRANCE) and India.Arie

"IRON LION ZION" with Ziggy Marley (JAMAICA) and ChocQuibTown

SERJ TANKIAN

Born in Lebanon to Armenian parents; migrated in 1975

★

Before he started a heavy metal thrasher band, Serj Tankian founded a software company.

Tankian, a self-professed late bloomer, didn't begin to play music or write songs until college, where he earned a business and marketing degree and started a vertical accounting software company.

But his passion for music grew, and he soon left the software business behind. He founded the Grammy-winning heavy metal band System of a Down in 1994, with friends who had attended the same bilingual Armenian parochial school in Los Angeles. His talent was evident from their first release. Tankian is a natural lyricist who frequently blends the personal and political. He has an unusually large range of 4.2 octaves—on par with vocalists like Freddie Mercury—and is routinely ranked as one of the greatest heavy metal singers of all time.

Tankian considers the life experiences he had before he came to music key factors in his current success. He now runs a record label, publishes poetry, and co-wrote a musical version of the ancient Greek tragedy *Prometheus Bound*, which was performed by the American Repertory Theater.

His political interests also transcend his lyrics; with Rage Against the Machine's Tom Morello, Tankian co-founded the nonprofit activist organization Axis of Justice to mobilize musicians and their fans in grassroots social justice initiatives. He is particularly passionate about Armenian politics, with much of his work centered on human rights and genocide prevention.

Just as Tankian and his bandmates have rejected critics' attempts to assign their music a specific genre, he sees no distinct difference between his work in the fields of music, politics, and technology.

For his next act, he's taken up painting.

SYSTEM OF A DOWN

ALBERTO VARGAS

Migrated from Peru via Europe in 1916

★

Legend has it that not long after he passed through Ellis Island, Alberto Vargas found himself in downtown Manhattan surrounded by beautiful women. It was lunchtime, and the city's office workers had streamed out onto Broadway—refined women Vargas considered to be the picture of sophistication. He decided then and there to make the beauty of American girls his next subject.

Vargas wasn't a trained painter—though he'd learned how to use an airbrush while retouching images for his photographer father, he was self-taught in the use of watercolor, a staple in much of his work. Starting in fashion illustration and movie posters, by the 1940s Vargas had been put under contract by *Esquire* to craft a series of more sensuous images. He painted hundreds of suggestively clad girls for the magazine, often stylizing their forms to emphasize their legs. His name quickly became synonymous with the pictures, which the magazine called "Varga Girls."

The paintings were wildly popular with readers and became the inspiration for much of the art featured on Allied World War II planes. But Varga Girls also angered defenders of a sexually conservative mainstream American culture—the U.S. Postal Service even took away *Esquire*'s second-class mailing permit in an attempt to shutter them. After a legal battle, Vargas moved on to *Playboy*.

His pinups would continue to meet conservative resistance, but Vargas never considered his work controversial. Rather than viewing them as obscene, he saw his paintings as a reverie, meant to celebrate women's poise and grace. He famously said, "What is more beautiful than a beautiful girl?" Today, his paintings are some of the bestselling in the world.

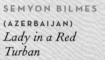

JOHN JAMES AUDUBON (BORN IN HAITI TO FRENCH PARENTS) *Birds of America*

SEMYON BILMES (AZERBAIJAN) *Lady in a Red Turban*

CHRISTO (BULGARIA) and JEANNE-CLAUDE (BORN IN MOROCCO TO FRENCH PARENTS) *The Gates*

ROBERT FRANK (SWITZERLAND) "Charleston, South Carolina" from *The Americans*

ULIKS GRYKA
(ALBANIA)
Sisyphus Stones

LADY PINK (ECUADOR)
Pink on a CC Train

JULIE MEHRETU
(ETHIOPIA)
Local Calm

ARSHILE GORKY
(ARMENIA)
Portrait of Ahko

MELEKO MOKGOSI
(BOTSWANA) from *Pax Kaffraria*

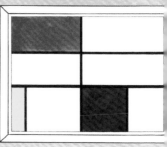

PIET MONDRIAN
(NETHERLANDS)
Composition in C

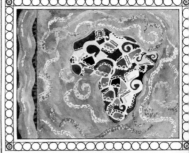

AÏDA TOURÉ (BORN IN
GABON TO GABONESE
AND MALIAN PARENTS)
The Luminous, the Coveted

SHIRIN NESHAT
(IRAN) *Untitled*

TAMARA DE LEMPICKA
(POLAND)
Young Lady with Gloves

FARAH AL QASIMI
(UNITED ARAB EMIRATES)
Self Portrait in Red

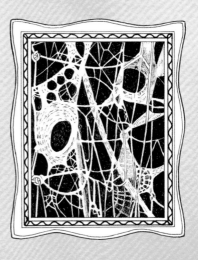

FAITH WILDING
(PARAGUAY)
*Close up of
Womb Room*

CARLO ALBÁN

Migrated from Ecuador in 1986

★

For five years, Carlo Albán hid his secret in plain sight. Each morning he'd appear on national television to play "Carlo," a version of himself, on *Sesame Street*. The wildly popular children's program uses a mix of live action, puppetry, and animation to represent a diverse range of American experiences, featuring characters of different backgrounds, abilities, and interests. Producers of the show didn't know it, but at the time, Albán was going through an experience that many viewers might have identified with, too, if only he had been allowed to talk about it: He was an undocumented immigrant, living in constant fear of deportation.

Albán was seven when he and his family arrived in the United States. As with most undocumented immigrants, they entered the country legally on temporary visas, but stayed after the visas' expiration. Though they were working with a lawyer to legally procure permanent residency, the process was constantly delayed. When Albán, by then a teenager, landed the role on *Sesame Street*, their status still hadn't been resolved. The paperwork he presented to the television network was all forged.

Despite a series of close calls on and off the *Sesame* set, Albán remained a beloved cast member and eventually got his green card. He'd go on to land roles on *Law & Order, Girls, Oz, Prison Break*, and *The Night Of* and star in the Broadway play *Sweat*.

Being an undocumented immigrant, he told *The Hype Magazine*, made him a better actor, because as an outsider he cultivated a heightened sense of cultural understanding. "I think as an actor your job is to put yourself in other people's shoes, and in order to do that you need to have a great deal of empathy for your characters, no matter who they are or where they come from."

MARCUS SAMUELSSON

Migrated from Ethiopia via Sweden in 1994

★

Marcus Samuelsson had been training for the head chef job at Aquavit, New York City's premiere Scandinavian restaurant, for most of his life.

He was born in Ethiopia on the cusp of the nation's civil war. When he was still a child, his mother died of tuberculosis, leaving him and his sister alone. The pair were adopted by a Swedish couple, from whom Marcus got his surname and an interest in cooking. His adopted mother was a terrible cook, but his grandmother Helga inspired him to pursue a career in food. He went on to study at the Culinary Institute in Gothenburg, and then in Switzerland and France.

When he took the job at Aquavit, he worried he'd tarnish its reputation. Instead, at twenty-three, he became the youngest chef ever to earn a three-star review from *The New York Times*.

Samuelsson worked on other top New York restaurant projects and won the television competition *Top Chef Masters*, but the September 11, 2001, attacks shifted his focus back to the importance of building community. He fixed his eyes on Harlem and began to plan his most famous restaurant to date—Red Rooster.

Striving to create both a destination dining experience and a staple of the neighborhood, Samuelsson prioritized affordability, local ingredients, and diverse cooking styles. "Food can be cooked from the soul," he told *The New York Times*, "but that doesn't make it soul food." Red Rooster specializes in what Samuelsson calls "American comfort food." Featuring everything from ramen to ceviche to chicken and waffles, the menu represents a mix of Harlem's varied cultures, including hints of Samuelsson's own Ethiopian and Swedish roots. "I want this to be a place where people from all walks of life break bread together," he said.

AMERICAN COMFORT FOOD

American cuisine has long been a product of its immigrants, and these comfort foods by talented chefs from around the world are no exception.

WOLFGANG PUCK (AUSTRIA) The Emmy-winning celebrity chef's take on schnitzel means thin pork cutlets deep-fried with panko bread crumbs and served with fingerling potatoes.

CRISTETA COMERFORD (PHILIPPINES) Lumpia, a crispy crepe-pastry wrapper filled with vegetables like chopped cabbage and bamboo, minced meat or shrimp, is a popular appetizer and street food. As White House executive chef, she frequently prepared the snack for the Obama family.

GORDON RAMSAY (UNITED KINGDOM) The fiery-tempered chef, who splits his time between California and London, is often seen on *MasterChef*, tutoring contestants in how to craft his signature beef Wellington: seasoned beef fillets wrapped in mushroom-coated Parma ham and baked in puff pastry, served with red wine sauce.

JOSÉ ANDRÉS (SPAIN) He recommends roasting paella—one of the most iconic Spanish dishes, featuring rice, meat, and seafood cooked with saffron—over an open flame in summertime.

PIERRE THIAM (SENEGAL) His take on fonio, a small-grain, gluten-free millet cereal, features cinnamon, brown sugar, fruit, toasted cashews, and almond milk, making it a hearty vegan breakfast.

KAMAL AND GEETA NIROULA (BHUTAN) This husband-and-wife team, who arrived in Utah as refugees fleeing ethnic cleansing in Bhutan, serve *ema datshi,* a popular cheese-and-chili-pepper stew, among other Bhutanese favorites, at their Salt Lake City restaurant.

SHYAM DAUSOA (MAURITIUS) His popular samosas, which he nicknamed "shyamosas," are fried pockets of spiced vegetables like potatoes, peas, or lentils, served with mint chutney. He also now makes vegan-friendly versions to serve his Portland clientele.

RAMIZ KUKAJ (KOSOVO) *Qebapa,* a garlicky mixed-meat sausage dish served with onion and pita, is a favorite not only at this chef's Bronx-based restaurant, Tradita, but all across the Balkans.

PIETRO FAETANINI (SAN MARINO) A new arrival in New York, he recently won Long Island's mixology competition by crafting a vodka martini featuring vanilla extract, orange juice, and smoked cotton candy.

DEFENDERS

ELIE WIESEL

Migrated from Romania via France in 1955

★

After Auschwitz, Elie Wiesel, who would go on to become the acclaimed author of more than fifty books, struggled with silence; he was disillusioned by the silence of the international community, who had allowed genocide on a massive scale to go on for years, and at the same time wished he himself could keep quiet and avoid reliving his own painful memories.

At fifteen he'd been deported to Auschwitz, then Buchenwald; his father, mother, and sister died in those camps. He arrived in France on an orphan transport and didn't speak about the Holocaust for a decade, until the writer François Mauriac encouraged him to write about his experience. Wiesel's first attempt was an outpouring of more than eight hundred pages: *And the World Remained Silent*. He'd rework it a few years later into the best-known memoir of the Holocaust, *Night*.

Still, he was ambivalent. For Wiesel, words could capture neither the horrors of the Holocaust nor the silence of its bystanders. "If I could communicate what I have to say through not publishing, I would do it," he said in an interview with Harry James Cargas. "If I could, to use a poetic image, communicate a Silence through silence I would do so. But I cannot."

The power of Wiesel's words, though, is undeniable: His body of work is credited with helping to standardize the meaning of the word *holocaust* itself. And, creative inhibitions aside, Wiesel never failed to speak up as an activist, work for which he won the Nobel Peace Prize.

"Whenever and wherever human beings endure suffering and humiliation, take sides. Neutrality helps the oppressor, never the victim. Silence encourages the tormentor, never the tormented," he said in his acceptance speech.

MIRIAM MAKEBA

Migrated from South Africa circa 1960

★

World-renowned musician and civil rights activist Miriam Makeba didn't consider her work political. Instead, she saw music as a method of communication for oppressed people, and a very personal expression of the painful experience of life under apartheid. "People say I sing politics," Makeba said while on her British tour in 1985. "But what I sing is not politics; it is the truth."

A civil rights advocate in both South Africa and the United States, Makeba was exiled from her home country for more than thirty years due to her anti-apartheid activism. So strong was her influence that the South African government canceled her passport, leaving her unable to return even for her mother's funeral. In America, Makeba was affiliated with the Pan-African, civil rights, and Black Power movements. When she married Stokely Carmichael, a Black Panther Party leader, she endured yet more hostility from white audiences as well as the U.S. government. The animosity caused her to move to Guinea, where she lived for fifteen years.

When she was allowed to return to South Africa, in 2000, it was as a UN Goodwill Ambassador; she lent her voice to support child-soldier rehabilitation, children with HIV and AIDS, and orphaned girls.

Despite division over her activism, Makeba's music has remained popular around the globe for decades. She brought African jazz, Afropop, and traditional South African music to large, sold-out venues in the United States, Europe, and Africa, and won a Grammy in collaboration with Harry Belafonte in 1966. But perhaps her best review would come from the former president of South Africa. Upon her death in 2008, Nelson Mandela said, "Her music inspired a powerful sense of hope in all of us."

MOHAMMAD SALMAN HAMDANI

Migrated from Pakistan in 1979

★

They say he saw the Twin Towers in flames from the elevated perch of the 7 train, which he rode each morning from Bayside, Queens, to Manhattan. He was a police cadet, an EMT, and a lab analyst at Rockefeller University's Howard Hughes Medical Institute. As a student, he wasn't required to respond to the emergency. He did so anyway.

Mohammad Salman Hamdani arrived in the United States at just thirteen months old. He grew up in Bayside, attending Catholic school, then playing football for Bayside High. Despite this all-American résumé, the media was quick to fan the flames of xenophobia when the twenty-three-year-old disappeared. Anonymous WANTED posters encouraged people with information to contact the police, while the *New York Post* ran the headline "Missing or Hiding?" All the while, Hamdani's body lay beneath the smoldering rubble of Ground Zero, his medical bag and identification badge alongside him.

Upon the discovery of his remains, authorities were quick to reverse the suspected-terrorism narrative, with the NYPD issuing full honors at his burial. Hamdani was enshrined in the Patriot Act as an exemplar of American bravery. In Bayside, 204th Street was named Salman Hamdani Way.

But Hamdani's name is not found among the first responders at the 9/11 Memorial & Museum—as a cadet and a volunteer, he technically did not die in the line of duty.

Nor, for murkier reasons, is he memorialized with others whose remains were uncovered at the North Tower. He is listed on the last panel among miscellaneous victims, those with no connections to the World Trade Center or NYPD units. His mother, a middle school English teacher in Queens, still speaks out in hopes that her son will be permanently recognized as the first responder that he was.

EVERYDAY HEROES

GUNNAR KAASEN (NORWAY) In 1925, when a diphtheria epidemic threatened northern Alaska and the port was frozen, he drove the last two legs of a dogsled relay through darkness and whiteout snow conditions to deliver three hundred thousand doses of antitoxin to Nome. His lead husky, considered by other mushers a second-stringer, was the famous Balto.

ANTONIO DÍAZ CHACÓN (MEXICO) He happened upon an abduction in progress when the kidnapper already had six-year-old Ashley in a van and was speeding away from the scene, trying to force her head down and away from the windows. Following the van until the kidnapper eventually lost control of the vehicle, Chacón carried the girl home and returned her to her mother. At the time, he was an undocumented immigrant.

CARLOS ARREDONDO (COSTA RICA) A spectator at the Boston Marathon in 2013, he was there to support a National Guard–linked organization that raised money for fallen soldiers' families; his own son, a marine, had been killed in Operation Iraqi Freedom. When the bombs went off, he sprung into action to help carry victims and move debris to make way for first responders.

WILLIAM RAMIREZ (COLOMBIA) One morning on his way to work, the Miami-based boat repairman saw a police officer lying down in the street and another man firing a rifle at him. He quickly parked his van between the officer and the perpetrator, pulled the officer into the side door of his van, and drove him to safety.

HYNES BIRMINGHAM (DOMINICA) When Hurricane Maria inflicted devastating structural damage over the majority of the island of his birth in 2017, he left his Connecticut home to serve with the International Medical Corps, providing emergency medical care to storm victims, many of whom were now homeless. This was his first trip back to the country he left at age four.

DAMBER SUBBA (BHUTAN) Raised in a refugee camp in Nepal after fleeing ethnic cleansing in Bhutan, his family was eventually relocated to Ohio. He became Akron's first refugee police officer in 2018, and now works to bridge cultural divides between the justice system and refugee communities.

DARLENE KEJU

Migrated from the Marshall Islands in 1967

★

The babies were see-through, boneless, and had no eyes. Some had no head, others had two. Most were stillborn, and those born alive lasted only a few hours. There was no word for the birth defects in Marshallese. They came to be known as "jellyfish babies."

Between 1946 and 1958, the U.S. government dropped sixty-seven nuclear bombs at several sites in the Marshall Islands as part of a nuclear testing initiative. One particularly large bomb, tested on Bikini Atoll in 1954, had 1,300 times the force of the one dropped on Hiroshima. While some Marshallese were evacuated, others—residents of nearby islands—were assured of their safety. The Marshallese people would experience a host of radiation-related health problems, including birth defects and cancer, for decades to come.

Born downwind of the Bikini Atoll testing site, Darlene Keju knew little about the effects of the United States' experiments until she arrived in Hawaii as a teenager. After studying public health at the University of Hawaii, she dedicated her life to educating fellow Marshallese, and the world, about the dangerous aftereffects of nuclear weaponry. She used music, dance, and skits to spread the word among young people on the islands. In the States and internationally, she delivered speeches railing against the U.S. government's repeated denial of the link between their testing and the Marshallese's health problems, and advocated for islander health- and resettlement programs.

Of the crusade she wrote, "We are only very small, very few thousand people out there on those tiny islands, but we are doing our part to stop this nuclear madness . . . which means you can do it too!"

She died of breast cancer in 1996, having just turned forty-five.

LUPITA NYONG'O

Migrated from Kenya in 2003

★

After winning an Oscar for her supporting-actress performance in the film *Twelve Years a Slave*, everyone wanted to lay claim to Lupita Nyong'o. Was she the first Kenyan Academy Award winner? The first female Mexican one? In an interview with *El Mañana*, she set the record straight once and for all: "I am Mexican-Kenyan, and I am fascinated by carne asada tacos."

Born in Mexico City to Kenyan parents, Nyong'o speaks of her multicultural upbringing with gratitude and no small dose of humor.

Nyong'o spent most of her childhood in a suburban community of Nairobi; she enjoyed theater from an early age, performing as Juliet with a Nairobi-based company when she was a teenager. When she was sixteen, her parents sent her back to Mexico so that she would gain Spanish fluency. This period, she told *Allure*, was "a bizarre, dire time for my hair"—though in the same breath she spoke of her love for Mexican culture and food; she routinely gives interviews with Latino news outlets in Spanish.

Beyond her jokes, the serious side of Nyong'o's candid nature made her an early force behind the #MeToo movement, when she wrote a *New York Times* op-ed about her sexual harassment at the hands of Harvey Weinstein, whom she encountered as a drama student. "Now that we are speaking, let us never shut up about this kind of thing," she wrote.

Today a warrior spy in *Black Panther* and the voice of a space creature in *Star Wars: Episode VIII—The Last Jedi*, Nyong'o has proven that her talent stretches across genres and media. One thing, though, hasn't changed: She says she still likes eating steak tacos before walking the red carpet.

THESE FEARLESS WOMEN FIGHT
FOR WOMEN'S RIGHTS IN THE
UNITED STATES AND AROUND THE WORLD.

SIMA WALI (AFGHANISTAN) An advocate for the rights and needs of women fleeing combat zones, she focused particularly on Afghani women's rights as CEO of the nonprofit Refugee Women in Development. She also served as vice president of the first international feminist think tank, the Sisterhood Is Global Institute, which consults with the United Nations to support women-centric education, policy, and infrastructure all over the world.

TANYA SELVARATNAM (SRI LANKA) A Portland, Oregon–based writer and artist, she was on the organizing committee of the NGO Forum/Fourth World Conference on Women in China, and worked as special projects coordinator for the Ms. Foundation, which invests in and amplifies women-led movements in the United States.

ZAINAB SALBI (IRAQ) At age twenty-three, she founded Women for Women International, an organization that seeks equality for women through economic self-sufficiency. The organization provides skills training, tools, and microcredit loans to women building small-business projects in the developing world.

EUDOXIE MBOUGUIENGUE BRIDGES (GABON) The wife of rapper Ludacris, she founded Unspoken Angels, a global domestic violence awareness organization that provides counseling, education, and supplies to survivors of verbal, physical, and sexual abuse in the United States and West Africa.

ZENAB HAMDAN (CHAD) She memorized the Quran by age twelve, and has since relocated to the Houston, Texas, area, where she tutors the women and girls of her local mosque in reading and memorizing the holy book. At 2014 Ramadan services, her students recited nighttime prayers publicly, a first for the area's Muslim community.

MAHA DAKHIL (LIBYA) A Creative Artists Agency talent agent when news of Harvey Weinstein's widespread abuses finally came to light, she was one of several high-powered women in the entertainment industry who organized to found the nonprofit Time's Up, which fights for safe and equal workplaces for women.

JAHA DUKUREH (GAMBIA) A survivor of female genital mutilation and forced child marriage, she grew up to be a Regional UN Women Ambassador for Africa, and founded the nonprofit Safe Hands for Girls, which combats FGM globally. She was nominated for a Nobel Peace Prize in 2018.

Z. ALEXANDER LOOBY

Migrated from Antigua in 1914

★

On the day his house exploded, Z. Alexander Looby was in the midst of legally representing 153 students arrested at Nashville area sit-ins and civil rights protests. A powerful bomb was detonated at his home in the dim hours of the morning. Though neither Looby nor his wife were harmed, the damage was vast, affecting neighboring buildings and blowing out nearly 150 windows at nearby Meharry Medical College.

In an interview, Looby tried to keep the peace, downplaying the destruction as an isolated incident. More than two thousand African Americans felt differently, taking to the streets of downtown Nashville to protest the bombing and the fact that no one had been arrested.

Looby had arrived in the United States at age fifteen, an orphan. He attended Howard University, Columbia Law School, and NYU, entering the public sphere as a lawyer for the NAACP. He sought acquittals for the men charged with attempted murder in the Columbia race riot of 1946, and fought for the desegregation of Nashville public schools. With this résumé of prominent work, he applied for membership in the Nashville Bar Association, but was rejected due to his race.

One month after the bombing and subsequent protests, Nashville lunch counters were desegregated, the first of any major southern city. Nashville's sit-ins became a model for other cities throughout the 1960s, and Looby continued fighting for civil rights in the South until his death in 1972.

Ten years later, the Nashville Bar Association accepted Looby as a posthumous member.

THE DOCTORS WHO SAVED PRESIDENT REAGAN'S LIFE

A rainy Monday afternoon in March outside of a Washington, D.C., Hilton hotel: John Hinckley, Jr., fired six shots at President Ronald Reagan, hitting him in the chest. Special agents pushed Reagan into his limo and directed the caravan to George Washington University Hospital. The president had been shot in the left lung, which collapsed from the wound, and the bullet barely missed his heart. While being wheeled into surgery, Reagan famously quipped to his doctors, "Please tell me you're Republicans."

What three of Reagan's doctors *were* were immigrants—his surgical anesthesia team was composed of resident MAY CHIN (MALAYSIA), GEORGE MORALES (NICARAGUA/MEXICO), and MANFRED LICHTMANN (GERMANY). Chin immigrated with her family as a child. Morales was sent from Nicaragua to Mexico as a young boy after his father made a dangerous judicial ruling against the nation's dictator. Lichtmann, a refugee of Nazi Germany, was raised in an American orphanage. As a result of the expert care provided by his team, Ronald Reagan became the first president to survive being shot while in office.

JAMIEL ALTAHERI

Migrated from Yemen circa 1986

The NYPD's first Yemeni American captain, and one of its highest-ranking Muslim officers, faces his biggest battles off-duty. While Jamiel Altaheri's record of service is full of impressive casework—including assisting the Bronx district attorney's office with a high-profile money-laundering case and a five-year undercover assignment with the Vice Enforcement Division—it's struggling to explain xenophobia to his young daughter that he considers his toughest assignment.

When his daughter returned from school to tell him about a bully who'd called her a terrorist, Altaheri was heartbroken, but stayed calm to discuss the power of words with her, reminding her to be proud of her identity as both a Muslim and an American.

It's a lesson he also teaches by example. He's the co-founder of the NYPD Muslim Officers Society, the founder of the Yemeni American Law Enforcement Officers Association, and routinely lectures at mosques, synagogues, churches, and schools about the dangers of hateful rhetoric. He made national news for lambasting candidates who scapegoated certain ethnic and religious groups during the 2016 election cycle. "One day she'll say, 'Dad, what did you do about it?'" he told CBS News of his efforts to curb the stigma against Islam. "At least I can respond back to her and say, 'Yes, daughter. I did something.'"

Altaheri has encountered his share of xenophobia during his day-to-day work as an officer, but there are also many people across the city who recognize his exceptional service. Said Bronx borough president Ruben Diaz, Jr., of Altaheri, "He exemplifies everything good that it means to be a Muslim, everything good that it means to be an immigrant, and everything good that it means to be an American."

TADEUSZ KOŚCIUSZKO

*Migrated from Belarus (then part of the
Polish-Lithuanian Commonwealth) via France in 1776*

Freedom was his career, and his legacy.

Living in France on the eve of the American Revolution, Tadeusz Kościuszko was intrigued by Thomas Jefferson, whom he'd met in Paris; moved by the Declaration of Independence; and generally interested in issues of human rights. In 1776, he set sail for the colonies with hopes of joining the American cause.

A skilled engineer, Kościuszko was welcomed and charged with designing and improving military fortifications for the Continental Army, a task he performed across the colonies. In 1778, George Washington commissioned him to design a fortification at West Point. Kościuszko spent more than two years on the project, its impenetrability later making it the new U.S. government's choice for the location of the nation's first military academy.

Kościuszko returned to Europe filled with revolutionary spirit, and there fought valiantly for Polish independence, though the movement ultimately collapsed without his leadership when he was captured and imprisoned.

Meanwhile, in America, he remained a hero, having been named brigadier general and granted U.S. citizenship for his service. He and Thomas Jefferson remained close friends and corresponded often, with Jefferson even being named the executor of Kościuszko's will.

Upon his death in 1817, Kościuszko's will stipulated that his American estate be sold, and the profits used to free and educate as many enslaved people as possible, including Jefferson's. Citing his own advanced age, Jefferson declined to execute the will, and the money was never used for its intended purpose.

AMERICAN WAR HEROES

Throughout the country's history, immigrants have been an integral part of the American armed forces. During World War I, about 18 percent of soldiers were foreign born. In 2016, 511,000 foreign-born veterans were living in the United States, while another 1.5 million vets had at least one immigrant parent.

CASIMIR PULASKI (POLAND) A war hero in both Poland and the United States, he was recruited by Benjamin Franklin to fight on the northern front in the American Revolutionary War. Leading a 1777 charge that arguably saved the life of George Washington, he was named brigadier general and came to be known as the "father of the American cavalry."

HI JOLLY (JORDAN) His origin story is somewhat murky, with people alternately citing Jordan, Syria, and Turkey as his place of birth, but he became well known in the States as one of the first camel drivers hired by the U.S. Army. At the helm of the U.S. Camel Corps as a trainer and breeder, he led the

Corps in completing several expeditions across the southwestern states, part of an initiative to use camels as cargo carriers for missions elsewhere.

FRANZ SIGEL (GERMANY) A military school graduate and lieutenant in the Baden Army, he immigrated to the United States, where he taught in New York City public schools until the outbreak of the American Civil War. Known in German-speaking communities for educating and recruiting immigrants to the cause of antislavery, he encouraged them to take up arms in the Civil War, where he served as major general in the Union Army.

ORLANDO CARUANA (MALTA) At the start of the American Civil War he enlisted in the Union Army; he was just seventeen, but told recruiters he was twenty. He was recognized for his valor at the Battle of New Bern and the Battle of South Mountain, for which he later received the Medal of Honor.

MATEJ KOCAK (SLOVAKIA) A U.S. Marine Corps sergeant in World War I, he heroically defended his battalion by rushing an enemy machine-gun nest alone with his bayonet, and then, later in that same battle,

organizing a company of French soldiers. For his actions he was awarded both the Navy and Army Medals of Honor.

JACOB C. VOUZA (SOLOMON ISLANDS) In 1942, after Japanese forces invaded Guadalcanal, the young marine volunteered to scout behind enemy lines. He was captured and tortured for hours; when he refused to give up any information, he was tied to a tree, stabbed, and left to die. He managed to free himself and return to warn the marines of an impending attack, and received the Silver Star and Legion of Merit for his service.

MICHAEL STRANK (SLOVAKIA) One of six World War II U.S. Marines who raised the flag on the top of Mount Suribachi and was immortalized in Joe Rosenthal's Pulitzer Prize–winning photograph, he was later killed in action during the Battle of Iwo Jima.

MACARIO GARCÍA (MEXICO) During a battle outside Grosshau, Germany, in 1944, he killed and captured several Nazi soldiers despite being wounded. He be-

came the first Mexican immigrant to receive the Medal of Honor.

JOSÉ GUTIÉRREZ (GUATEMALA) He arrived in America in the mid-1990s—orphaned, undocumented, and with dreams of being an architect. By 2002, he was a permanent U.S. resident and had put his college plans on hold to serve his new country. He enlisted with the marines and was deployed to Iraq, where he died in 2003. He is thought to have been the second U.S. serviceman killed in the Iraq War.

ALIO NAALLAH (NIGER) Arriving in the States at sixteen, he practiced English by watching *Wheel of Fortune*. He joined the military as an expression of gratitude to his new country, and served as an airman turned military financial analyst. He earned an MBA in international business during his time in the air force.

LOUISA BENSON CRAIG

Migrated from Myanmar (then Burma) in 1967

★

For most people, competing in beauty pageants and fighting in bloody ethnic wars are mutually exclusive. But for Louisa Benson Craig, they were both acts of rebellion.

Craig was ten when her mother entered her into her first pageant as part of a plan to endear the district commissioner's wife to her family. It worked; so enraptured was the powerful woman by Craig's unconventional Jewish-Karen looks that Craig's father, a rebel, was released from prison.

Though she was part of the Karen ethnic minority the Burmese government scorned, Craig's status as a beauty icon won her the favor of many of her future enemies. She was crowned in two Miss Burma pageants and was Burma's first Miss Universe contestant, but none of it came naturally. High heels and posing, she'd later tell her daughter, the novelist Charmaine Craig, were "a nuisance."

By the time Craig met her first husband, Brigadier General Lin Htin of the Karen National Liberation Army, he had a bullet in his skull and had already been erroneously declared dead several times. When he disappeared in the jungle and was once again believed to be deceased, the KNLA's Fifth Brigade looked to his widow for leadership. Craig cut her hair and led the brigade, taking on key roles in several negotiations with enemy generals and always turning down villagers' offers of women's clothing.

After moving to America to marry a former Tufts classmate, Craig remained an activist for refugees and built a quiet life that suited her personality. But by then her story had outgrown her, taking on its own mythological force: Karen legend has it she is still in the jungle, where she rides a white horse and watches over her people.

EUGENIA FORTES

Migrated from Cape Verde in 1920

★

Arriving in New Bedford, Massachusetts, on a schooner jam-packed with new immigrant families, nine-year-old Eugenia Fortes was quick to discover that racism was not, as many liked to believe, contained by the Mason-Dixon Line. "Well, America has a down South, but it also has an up South," she said in an interview with the New Bedford *Standard-Times*.

After high school, Fortes struggled to find work. Once, on a trip into Boston, she was turned away from the YWCA on racial grounds. Seeing firsthand that discrimination was alive in New England, she decided she would make it her life's work to combat the racism locals would prefer to say didn't exist.

She spent most of her life on the predominantly white peninsula of Cape Cod, where she worked as a housekeeper, then as a cook in a school cafeteria. In 1945 she staged her own sit-in on Hyannis Port's East Beach, which was segregated. When the police approached her and asked her to leave the "white" area, she refused on the grounds that, since the beach was public, everyone should have equal access to it. Fortes later fought against privatization of that stretch of beach in order to prevent the implementation of further discriminatory regulations.

By 1961, she'd helped found Cape Cod's chapter of the NAACP, and often hosted Justice Thurgood Marshall and his family at her home. When civil rights demonstrations occurred in the area, Edward Kennedy looked to Fortes to help form his report for the president on the state of things "up South."

Fortes continued to serve the Cape, on the board of directors for the Hyannis library, as a Red Cross volunteer, and as a member of the Massachusetts and U.S. civil rights commissions. In 2004, East Beach was renamed for her, and today anyone can visit Eugenia Fortes Beach.

GET UP, STAND UP: AMERICAN ACTIVISTS

WONG CHIN FOO (CHINA) The first to coin the term *Chinese American*, he spent his time on a lecture circuit educating people about Chinese customs and religion to combat rampant anti-Chinese xenophobia, and founded the Chinese Equal Rights League to fight the Chinese Exclusion Act of 1882.

MARY HARRIS "MOTHER" JONES (IRELAND) A community organizer and co-founder of the Industrial Workers of the World union, she led strikes to protest child labor and coal-mine and silk-mill worker conditions. Once, when she was arrested and put on trial for a particularly large miner's strike in West Virginia, the district attorney called her "the most dangerous woman in America."

JACOB RIIS (DENMARK) This turn-of-the-century journalist shed light on the harrowing conditions of the New York City slums in his book *How the Other Half Lives*. The popular work is cited as one of the reasons behind early NYC tenement reform laws.

YELENA BONNER (TURKMENISTAN) A human rights activist for the Soviet Union's political prisoners as early as the 1940s, she was known for her criticism of Russia's authoritarian practices, particularly the government's treatment of the Chechen people. In her later years, she wrote frequently against Vladimir Putin and split her time between Russia and America.

STOKELY CARMICHAEL (TRINIDAD AND TOBAGO) A writer and civil rights activist, he was one of the original Freedom Riders who engaged in civil disobedience to protest segregated public buses in the southern United States. He was also a prominent member of the Black Panther Party and the Student Nonviolent Coordinating Committee.

VAMIK VOLKAN (CYPRUS) An acclaimed professor and scholar of psychiatry, he studies transmission of trauma across generations, societal mourning, and psychoanalysis between disparate cultures. Using his research, he founded the International Dialogue Initiative to bring people from conflicting nations and cultures into conversation with one another. He's been nominated for the Nobel Peace Prize four times.

NAGI DAIFULLAH (YEMEN) As a young farmworker in California, he became an organizer and strike captain for the United Farm Workers labor union in the 1970s. Trilingual, he used his skills to unite laborers across ethnic and linguistic boundaries.

MATHILDE KRIM (ITALY) A leading cancer researcher at the Sloan-Kettering Institute for much of her career, she dedicated her focus to AIDS research when news of the first cases began breaking in the early 1980s. She established several AIDS-related medical foundations, including the American Foundation for AIDS Research (amfAR), and in 2000 was awarded the Presidential Medal of Freedom for her work.

GILBERT TUHABONYE (BURUNDI) The survivor of a gruesome massacre in the Burundian civil war, he later arrived in the United States via the Olympic training program. A long-distance runner, he carried the Olympic torch in the 1996 relay through Birmingham, Alabama. He's now a public speaker on genocide awareness, and founder of the Gazelle Foundation, which strives to support unity among different ethnic and tribal groups in Burundi.

BERNARD CHERKASOV (AZERBAIJAN) Once a teenage refugee, he's now the CEO of the nonprofit Cradles to Crayons, an organization that provides underserved kids with school supplies, clothes, shoes, arts and crafts materials, and birthday presents in Chicago, Philadelphia, and Boston.

IDA LJUNGQVIST (TANZANIA) The first African-born woman to be named *Playboy* Playmate of the Year in 2009, she has worked extensively with the think tank Empowerment Works, a global initiative that gives people in developing nations access to education and economically and environmentally sustainable technology.

JOCELYN HOWARD (MICRONESIA) As the program director for the organization We Are Oceania, she helps combat homelessness, unemployment, lack of healthcare, and high rates of incarceration of minors for Micronesian immigrants in the United States, particularly within Hawaii.

KUSHABA MOSES MWOREKO (UGANDA) Fleeing death threats and incarceration, he was recently granted asylum in the United States, where he writes and speaks on LGBTQ rights for people around the world. He was a strong opponent of Uganda's proposed (and nulli-

fied) Anti-Homosexuality Act, which would have imposed life imprisonment or the death penalty as punishment for gay relationships.

JELICA BRUER NUCCIO (CROATIA) The first DeafBlind director of the Seattle DeafBlind Service Center, she works to ensure access to education, employment, and support services for the DeafBlind community nationwide. She is an advocate for and linguistics consultant on Protactile ASL, a burgeoning new language in the Deaf-Blind community.

MONA HANNA-ATTISHA (BORN IN THE UNITED KINGDOM TO IRAQI PARENTS) Born to dissident parents who'd fled Saddam Hussein's regime, she risked her career in medicine to draw attention to the high levels of lead she'd noticed in her young patients' blood, exposing the Flint, Michigan, water crisis in the process.

PRERNA LAL (FIJI) Once an undocumented student, they are now a top immigration attorney, law professor, and LGBTQ rights activist in California and globally, and one of the founders of DreamActivist, a grassroots advocacy network that uses social media to connect and advocate for undocumented minors.

THERESE PATRICIA OKOUMOU (DEMOCRATIC REPUBLIC OF THE CONGO) Angered by the separation of families and the detention of minors at the U.S.-Mexico border, she staged a Fourth of July protest noticed around the world when she scaled the Statue of Liberty in 2018. She was found guilty of several federal charges and sentenced to five years' probation and two hundred hours of community service.

FRANCIS BOK

Migrated from South Sudan in 1999

★

Francis Bok was seven years old when he was kidnapped during a violent militia raid of a village where he was selling eggs and peanuts for his mother. This was a common occurrence during the Second Sudanese Civil War, a decades-long conflict that would ultimately leave roughly two million people dead and four million displaced. Amid the raid's carnage, Bok was strapped to the back of a militia member's donkey. He'd never been to school and could count only to ten. It would become a fateful number for him—he'd spend ten years of his life enslaved.

For the next decade, Bok was the property of a northern Sudanese family. Routinely beaten, he was forced to care for, and sleep with, the family's cattle, perform other domestic and farm labor, eat spoiled food, and adopt an Arabic name and Islamic prayer practices.

When he finally broke free at age seventeen and sought help at a nearby police station, the police enslaved him for two months. When he again escaped and made it to the capital, Khartoum, he'd spend another seven months in jail for speaking out about his bondage; the government enforced a strict policy of denying that slavery existed.

Rescued by the United Nations and resettled in North Dakota, he found a softer strain of denial was prevalent in his new home. There, no one had heard of slavery—at least not in the context in which Bok spoke of it, as an active institution still wreaking havoc on millions of lives. Often, people he met would respond with surprise and even incredulity.

He'd go on to make abolitionism his life's work, collaborating with the American Anti-Slavery Group and Sudan Sunrise to raise awareness of modern slavery. In 2000, he would become the first escaped slave to testify before the U.S. Senate Committee on Foreign Relations.

PETER FRANCISCO

Migrated from Portugal in 1765

★

The Virginia Giant. The Virginia Hercules. The Giant of the Revolution. One of America's first war heroes, Peter Francisco accrued these nicknames not only for his stature but for the extent of his bravery as a soldier in the American Revolution.

But before he was Hercules, he was a lost boy. Believed to have been abducted from the Portuguese Azores, he was found at age five abandoned at the wharf in City Point, Virginia. He spoke no English and could not name the country from which he'd come. Taken in by colonists and raised in the spirit of the burgeoning revolution, he was said to be listening through a window outside the Second Virginia Convention in 1775 when Patrick Henry famously declared, "Give me liberty, or give me death!"

By this point, Francisco was fifteen, brawny, and itching to fight for the cause. At six feet six and more than 250 pounds, he was a foot taller than the average colonial man. He joined the army a year later, and was a formidable figure on the battlefield from the start, famed for his extra-long sword. In 1779, he was one of twenty soldiers handpicked by Washington for the assault on Stony Point. According to Captain William Evans, Francisco— who'd continued in battle despite a bayonet wound—was the picture of valor, for which "his name was reiterated throughout the whole army."

The next year, in Camden, South Carolina, Francisco would perform perhaps his most famous act: During an assault that had the Continentals outnumbered and retreating, Francisco ran into the field and single-handedly carried an 1,100-pound cannon on his back to Continental territory. A painting of Francisco with a cannon on his shoulder and the words *Fighter Extraordinary* were later featured on a bicentennial postage stamp.

FOREIGN SERVICE:
NONCITIZENS IN THE MILITARY

Immigrants have long made up a significant part of the U.S. armed forces, but foreign nationals also frequently serve our military.

Many of these foreign soldiers join under the Compact of Free Association, an agreement with the Federated States of Micronesia, Palau, and the Marshall Islands. The United States uses island space for military bases in exchange for protection, and citizens of those countries can serve in the U.S. armed forces. Pacific Islanders often speak of a feeling of patriotism and gratitude toward the United States for its defense from Japan during World War II as a reason to serve, and see it as a valuable employment opportunity.

But the phenomenon of foreign nationals serving in the U.S. military is not only a Pacific Islands story. Citizens from countries around the globe turn to American military service as a means of economic and educational opportunity. Many also see the military as a path to permanent residency or citizenship in the United States, though the current administration has sought to curb this practice, discharging noncitizens as "security risks."

The Department of Defense notes that approximately twenty-four thousand noncitizens were on active duty as of 2012.

JOSEPH PULITZER (HUNGARY) Before he became a newspaper mogul and the namesake for the Pulitzer Prize, he secured passage to the States by enlisting in the Union Army as a substitute for an American draftee. He served for a year in the Lincoln Cavalry.

PASIFIKA FALANI (TUVALU) During World War II, the U.S. Marines relied on local intelligence to navigate unfamiliar Pacific waters. Falani, a Tuvaluan civil servant, was one of the first islanders to have extensive contact with American forces, and is best remembered for performing recon missions and guiding American fleets through reefs and lagoons to their main base on Funafuti.

JASPER OBAKRAIRUR (PALAU) An army sergeant who joined up in hopes of finding a better life, he was killed by a roadside bomb outside Kabul, Afghanistan, in 2009. A tiny island with a population of just under twenty-two thousand, Palau sends more people into the U.S. armed forces per capita than the United States itself.

SAPURO NENA (MICRONESIA) A Kosraean native who joined the U.S. Army in search of opportunity and adventure, he earned multiple commendations and achievement medals during his service, and was remembered as constantly studying and working toward promotion. The sergeant deployed to Afghanistan with the Second Battalion in 2011, and was killed in action in September 2012, alongside four of his fellow soldiers.

MOVERS

PEDRO MARTÍNEZ

Migrated from the Dominican Republic in 1992

★

In Manoguayabo, they pitched with oranges or the heads of their sisters' dolls. The fifth of six children, Pedro Martínez grew up idolizing his older brother, who was training at the Dodgers' Dominican baseball academy. Martínez tagged along to carry his brother's bag. Once, after practice, his older brother clocked Pedro's pitches at 80 miles per hour. He was fourteen.

Making his major league debut in 1992, Martínez was small for a pitcher, especially one facing juiced-up home run machines like Sammy Sosa and Mark McGwire. But that didn't stop the eight-time all-star from maintaining one of the lowest earned run averages in baseball history. The first Latin American pitcher to achieve a career three thousand strikeouts, he won three Cy Young Awards and was a 2015 Hall of Fame shoo-in.

On the mound, Martínez's arm and attitude were feared. Commanding five different pitches, he was often unhittable. He talked smack about Babe Ruth and inspired several bench-clearing brawls, one in which he pushed Yankees coach Don Zimmer to the ground.

But there was a reason behind his bravado. "When I went on the mound, I felt like a lion fighting for my food," he told *The New York Times*, "because I wasn't fighting for myself. I was fighting for everyone in Manoguayabo."

Back home, he funded the construction of more than forty houses, a school, a day care, two churches, and paved roads. In a place where baseball is seen as kids' only ticket out, Martínez's foundation emphasizes music and English education, provides computers, combats domestic violence, and awards individual scholarships. One sent a young woman to Boston to study journalism; in 2005, she became Martínez's wife. Her husband, she told *The Boston Globe*, is "a bit of a softie."

RIHANNA

Migrated from Barbados in 2004

★

Robyn Rihanna Fenty grew up in a bungalow in Bridgetown, selling clothing with her father in a street stall. Her father's alcoholism and drug addiction cast long shadows over her childhood; she got headaches—strong ones, so bad doctors thought she had a brain tumor. Her health improved upon her parents' divorce. She was fourteen, and nothing had yet signaled that her life would be extraordinary.

Later, in an interview with *GQ*, Rihanna told the magazine she always wanted to finish high school, but that she "got busy." Finishing high school is perhaps the only thing Rihanna hasn't done. The diversity of her sound, lyrics, and looks can give the impression that she's lived multiple lives. Certainly, she's achieved enough for multiple people.

She was fifteen and singing in a girl group with two of her classmates when she was discovered by American record producer Evan Rogers while he was on vacation. Rogers invited her to the States soon after to record a demo, and by the time she was seventeen her debut single had hit number two on the *Billboard* Hot 100. She won her first Grammy at age twenty, and was two weeks shy of her twenty-first birthday when she was thrust into the spotlight as a victim of domestic violence—a tumult of media coverage some thought would threaten her teen superstar brand. But she made it through, and the best was yet to come.

Before she was thirty, Rihanna had nine Grammys and six Guinness World Records and was named the Harvard Foundation's 2017 Humanitarian of the Year. Alongside other philanthropic work, she recently funded the establishment of a state-of-the-art breast cancer detection and treatment center in her hometown hospital.

When she returns to Barbados to visit, her family just calls her Robyn.

From the mountains to the prairies / To the oceans white with foam / God bless America, my home sweet home.

—IRVING BERLIN

(RUSSIA) "GOD BLESS AMERICA"

Everybody here's gonna have some fun / Doin' the mess around.

—AHMET ERTEGUN

(TURKEY) CO-FOUNDER AND
PRESIDENT OF ATLANTIC RECORDS,
AND WRITER AND PRODUCER OF
"MESS AROUND" SUNG BY
RAY CHARLES

You've got to roll with the punches to get to what's real.

—VAN HALEN

(FEATURING BROTHERS
EDDIE AND ALEX VAN HALEN OF
THE NETHERLANDS) "JUMP"

Get on your feet / Get up and make it happen.
——PERFORMED BY
GLORIA ESTEFAN
(CUBA) "GET ON YOUR FEET"

Celebrate we will / Because life is short but sweet for certain.
——DAVE MATTHEWS
(SOUTH AFRICA) "TWO STEP"

East Coast to West Coast and everything in between / This is dedicated to everybody chasing their dreams.
——IMMORTAL TECHNIQUE
(PERU) "THE GETAWAY"

I'm in my own lane; you ain't in my category.
——PERFORMED BY
NICKI MINAJ
(TRINIDAD AND TOBAGO)
"HOV LANE"

MEB KEFLEZIGHI

Migrated from Eritrea via Italy in 1987

★

It had long been Meb Keflezighi's instinct to run. Growing up surrounded by Eritrea's bloody war for independence, he ran from the carnage of bodies and land mines. When his family fled to Italy and he saw a television for the first time, he rushed to see the back side of the set, wondering how actors could fit into such a small box; that same year he saw his first car and ran into the bushes to hide, sure it was a harbinger of death.

Still, he was an unlikely pick for athletic stardom; he didn't run competitively until he arrived in the United States at age twelve. His first race? A challenge from his gym teacher: Anyone who could run a mile in under six minutes and fifteen seconds would automatically get an A. He later excelled as a runner at UCLA, but when he completed his first marathon—the 2002 New York City race—he vowed never to do it again.

Yet when the pain faded, he was once again drawn to the challenge of long-distance running. By 2004, he'd run an Olympic marathon in Athens and won a silver medal for Team USA. In 2009 he became the first American to win the NYC Marathon since 1982.

He was sidelined with an injury for the fateful 2013 Boston Marathon; he remembers the explosions and being shoved into a hotel during the chaos. Galvanized by patriotism and love for his sport, he vowed to run in the 2014 event.

The morning of the marathon, reporters focused their questions on Keflezighi's retirement plans. Undeterred, he crossed the finish line with an eleven-second lead and his personal best time. At thirty-eight, he was the oldest Boston Marathon winner since 1930, and the first American to win since 1983. He is the only athlete ever to win the Boston and NYC marathons and an Olympic medal.

ANDRÉS CANTOR

Migrated from Argentina in the late 1970s

★

His mother arrived in Argentina from Romania at age thirteen. His father was already there, his grandparents having fled Nazi occupation in Poland years earlier. But for Americans who encounter him on the world stage as a sportscaster for Univision, there is no one more representative of Argentinian spirit than Andrés Cantor.

To shout "Goooooooooooooooal!" after a score in a soccer match is not an invention of Cantor's, nor of any announcer's—it's the sound of households across Latin America, a way to call nearby friends and family back to the radio or screen. But it's Cantor who brought the exclamation stateside, and who imbues it with a joy so relatable, it quickly became inextricable from him.

In Spanish, *cantor* refers to a singer, in English, the leader of a prayer. In a way Cantor is an amalgam of these things; his dramatic vocal performances and fervent devotion to the sport have drawn audiences into soccer games for more than thirty years, his persona mythologized in sports broadcasting.

Cantor's famous bellow is now mimicked across American sports television and radio, but there is no replacement for the charisma of the original; in the movie *Muppets Most Wanted* and on *The Simpsons*, Cantor plays himself.

TSIDII LE LOKA

Migrated from Lesotho in the 1990s

★

In Disney's 1994 animated hit movie *The Lion King*, Rafiki is a man. More precisely, he's a male baboon, one who offers encouragement to the lion prince, Simba, but is otherwise a secondary character, there as much for the laughs over his bright-red butt as he is for spiritual guidance.

Julie Taymor, director of *The Lion King* stage musical, had different plans for the play. Advocating for a return to the true African spirit of the story—relatively neutered in the film— meant ensuring that the cast always had a certain number of South African performers in the rotation who were familiar with the Zulu, Swahili, Xhosa, and Sesotho languages. It also meant finding a strong female lead in a male-dominated story.

Taymor began hearing murmurings of a talented young performer from Lesotho when Tsidii Le Loka was just an undergraduate at the University of Massachusetts at Amherst. Growing up in the small kingdom within South Africa, Le Loka had already found singing success at home, but she'd never been on Broadway. When she auditioned, Taymor knew she had found a star.

Le Loka originated the role of Rafiki in its new form—a spiritual hub of the savannah community, part royal council, part soothsayer. In addition to embodying the role's increased metaphysical gravitas, she was also the only cast member to contribute to the soundtrack, composing the Zulu song "Rafiki Mourns" for the Grammy-winning album. Her performance was hailed as one of the best-ever Broadway debuts. In 1998, she was nominated for a Tony and won a Drama Desk Award.

While Le Loka elevated her character from buffoon to an integral part of the *Lion King* kingdom, she herself had long been royalty even off the stage: A descendant of the amaHlubi king Langalibalele, she is a traditional Bantu princess.

PLAYBILL

LEE STRASBERG (AUSTRIA-HUNGARY, NOW POLAND) A stage actor in his earlier years, he truly claimed the spotlight as a teacher. He is considered the father of method acting in America, and served as a director for the prestigious nonprofit Actors Studio school in New York City.

MARLENE DIETRICH (GERMANY) Known for her self-reinventions, she transitioned from theater into film, then returned to the stage in her later years, touring the nation in her own popular cabaret act. Often she'd perform the first half of her show in a sexy gown, the second in a top hat and tails.

GERALDINE FITZGERALD (IRELAND) Successful in both Hollywood and NYC, this Broadway starlet was, in 1982, one of the first women to be nominated for a Tony for Best Direction of a Play. She also won an Emmy and earned a star on the Hollywood Walk of Fame.

PLAYBILL

MOISÉS KAUFMAN (VENEZUELA)
Founder of the Tectonic Theater Project, he's most famous for co-writing the groundbreaking play *The Laramie Project*.

DAPHNE RUBIN-VEGA (PANAMA) Her theater career began as a comedian with the troupe El Barrio USA, but she is best known for originating the role of Mimi in Jonathan Larson's acclaimed musical drama *Rent*. Working with Larson to develop the character from the show's initial workshop, she was nominated for a Tony and won a Theatre World Award.

TREVOR NOAH (SOUTH AFRICA) He was born in Johannesburg of an interracial relationship for which his mother was imprisoned under apartheid. His stand-up comedy often deals with race and identity, his shows so successful that he earned a spot on Comedy Central as host of *The Daily Show with Trevor Noah*.

GENE SIMMONS

Migrated from Israel in 1958

★

He arrived in New York City as Chaim Witz, age eight, the picture of a nice Jewish boy. Witz, whose name was changed to Gene shortly after his arrival, was the only child of a doting single mother and Holocaust survivor, Flora. He spoke Hebrew, Hungarian, and German, enjoyed reading comics and science fiction—even publishing his own fanzines—and attended yeshiva in Brooklyn before transferring to public school in Queens. He went on to study education, taught sixth grade in Harlem, and was an editorial assistant at *Vogue* and *Glamour*. He was an excellent typist.

He'd always been a talented musician, but it would take a face full of stage makeup to mask his good-boy ways and transform him into the founder of and bassist for the rock band KISS. Upon entering the music industry he changed his surname to Simmons, but fans would come to know him as Demon.

The divide between Simmons's early and adult lives feels as stark as the high-contrast face paint he made iconic. Onstage, the Demon breathes fire, vomits fake blood, flaunts his sexuality, and is famous for his extra-long tongue, so famous, in fact, he leveraged its notoriety to create his own men's magazine, *Gene Simmons Tongue*.

But perhaps a little of the old Chaim Witz exists in KISS after all—their outlandish look is a mash-up of the cartoon, comic-book, and sci-fi aesthetics he loved as a boy.

IMAN

Migrated from Somalia via Kenya in 1975

★

At nineteen, while walking to class at the University of Nairobi, Iman was stopped on the street by the photographer Peter Beard, who asked her if she'd ever had her photo taken. She dismissed him at first, and remembers thinking, "Oh God, here we go, another white man who thinks Africans have never seen a camera before." When Iman replied that of course, her parents had taken her picture, Beard offered to pay for the chance to photograph her. She agreed, requesting the exact amount of her upcoming tuition bill.

When she traveled to the United States a year later, it was accompanied by an outlandish tale of African exoticism: Beard said he'd discovered her tending five hundred cattle and sheep in a Kenyan game preserve. Her real-life story would've been powerful enough. She was born poor to teen parents. Her family worked hard to rise through the ranks of Somali society, but during the country's civil war was forced to flee on foot across the border to Kenya in the middle of the night.

Initially Iman agreed to play along with Beard's concocted biography, but her cosmopolitan nature and ability to speak five languages quickly upended the story. Still, she didn't need theatrics to draw the attention of the biggest names in fashion; her beauty quickly propelled her to supermodel status, and she became a muse for designers like Yves Saint Laurent, who called her his "dream woman." She has earned a premium for her modeling work, runs a multimillion-dollar cosmetics business, and is a prominent philanthropist. In 1992 she married David Bowie, whose name she still wears on a pendant around her neck.

Now sixty-three, Iman never quite shook the exotic aura of her fake origin story; her looks continue to be described as extraordinary and rare. She, however, insists she has typical Somali features.

MIKHAIL BARYSHNIKOV

Migrated from Latvia (formerly part of the U.S.S.R.) via Canada in 1975

★

On the evening of his defection from the Soviet Union, Mikhail Baryshnikov was late for his own getaway.

A member of the Kirov Ballet, Baryshnikov had temporarily joined the touring company of the Bolshoi Ballet in Toronto after other dancers had been double-booked. At the time, he had no plan for defecting, but when someone at the opening-night gala passed him a phone number, he learned that someone would be waiting to help him after the show. He hesitated. The escape would be difficult to pull off; Baryshnikov and his fellow dancers were constantly minded by KGB guards, who controlled their comings and goings.

Already an international star, Baryshnikov had access to all the creature comforts he desired at home. But the Russian ballet world was conservative, eschewing musicality for technical perfection, with no patience for the study of contemporary dance. Longing for creative freedom, he decided to take the chance.

The night's performance ran late, in part because his closing number was so excellent, his curtain-call applause was prolonged. Afterward, when Soviet agents were ushering the dancers back onto buses, Baryshnikov disappeared into a crowd of autograph seekers, then took off running. A getaway vehicle brought him into the countryside to wait for his asylum paperwork.

The Bolshoi Ballet had long promoted the Soviet Union as a pillar of modern culture. Baryshnikov's defection was a devastating blow to that image amid the Cold War climate.

Baryshnikov migrated to the United States, where he danced with the American Ballet Theatre and the New York City Ballet, as well as with contemporary greats like Twyla Tharp and Alvin Ailey. Following the breakup of the Soviet Union, he was awarded Latvian citizenship, his creative genius recognized at home once more.

THE WORLD OF DANCE

SOULEYMANE BADOLO (BURKINA FASO) An award-winning dancer and choreographer, he combines African and Western contemporary movement in his work, and teaches music students to explore connections between dance and percussion. On a visit home to Burkina Faso, he was part of anti-military protests that helped reinstate the country's electoral process.

SIDIKI CONDE (GUINEA) At age fourteen, after contracting polio and losing the use of his legs, he was exiled from his family's village, as was customary for disabled people. Knowing that his coming-of-age ceremony was approaching, and that he would lose his connection with his community if he could not participate in the traditional dance reflective of the transition from boy to man, Conde worked hard to re-create the choreography to be performed on his hands. Later, he founded Message d'Espoir, an orchestra of disabled street musicians, and became a soloist and rehearsal master for the West African dance company Les Merveilles de Guinée, touring with both groups. Upon arriving in New York City in 1998, Conde created the Tokounou All-Abilities Dance and Music Ensemble, which performs around the world today. He also teaches dance and music workshops in city schools.

GEORGE BALANCHINE (RUSSIA) The son of a composer, he was known for his musicality and the mash-up of styles he created by drawing from his work with the Mariinsky Theatre Ballet Company, on Broadway, and in Hollywood. The result was a more expressive and athletic ballet technique than its predecessors and set the standard for modern American ballet today. In 1933, he created the School of American Ballet to ensure that dancers were trained to his specifications, then founded the New York City Ballet to carry out more than four hundred works of his choreography. Known perhaps most of all as a teacher, Balanchine encouraged collaboration between artists, dancers, composers, and designers and urged them to think innovatively about movement and space.

RAFAEL ARUTYUNYAN

Migrated from Georgia (formerly part of the U.S.S.R.) in 2000

★

Though he's loved skating since he was a young boy, Coach Arutyunyan doesn't love his figure skaters. Known as a technician and "jump specialist," he has coached skaters to World, U.S. Championship, and Olympic titles since the early 1980s, when he trained a student who placed sixth in the Junior World Championships before he had even had any formal teacher training himself.

The relationship between Arutyunyan and his skaters is intense, and the coach is not one to mince words or soften corrections. In an interview with the Russian *Sports Daily*, he said he frequently asks his skaters, "Do you want compliments, or do you want to skate well?"

The emotional line he draws between himself and his skaters is not just a performance of toughness, but what he sees as a correction of a common error in the figure skating world, where coaches treat their skaters like their own children (sometimes, parents *are* coaches). "There should be no love, only respect," he explained to *Sports-Express*, another Russian news outlet. Respect, he says, minimizes tensions between skaters, because they feel Arutyunyan treats them equally. Keeping it professional between coach and skater also prevents blowups, rash decisions, and injuries.

It appears Arutyunyan's tough (non-)love has paid off; his mentees are some of American figure skating's most adored champions, including Michelle Kwan, Adam Rippon, and Nathan Chen. Chen, the 2018 world champion and Olympic bronze medalist, has soared particularly high under the guidance of the jumpmaster: He's the only competitive skater with the ability to execute five different kinds of quadruple jumps.

ENRIQUE IGLESIAS

Migrated from Spain circa 1982

The king of Latin pop wasn't interested in maintaining the family dynasty. The youngest son of international singing star Julio Iglesias, Enrique could have easily entered the music world on the weight of his last name. Instead, determined to be successful on his own, he made a demo under a pseudonym, pretending to be from Central America. He didn't tell his parents until after he'd signed the record deal.

Born in Spain in 1975, Iglesias was sent to Miami to live with his father at age seven, out of worry for his safety after his grandfather was kidnapped by Basque terrorists. With his father on tour for long stretches, Iglesias found solace in writing music and in his nanny, Elvira. When he needed money to record his demo, she lent it to him. He'd later dedicate his first album to her.

Now Iglesias frequently tops the *Billboard* charts, and is one of the most successful crossover artists ever, having sold more than 170 million albums worldwide. But he has none of the natural inclinations of the king or the hero, at least with respect to his ego. While his father claimed to have slept with upward of three thousand women, Iglesias continues to sing the praises of his longtime partner, tennis star Anna Kournikova, with whom he had twins in 2017. "Anna is the coolest girl I've ever known," he told the *Evening Standard*, "because she's the kind of girl you can take to McDonald's." He hates having his photo taken, speaks candidly about his anxiety about doing well, and finds the attention from fans more perplexing than gratifying. "You wake up in the morning, and you say, 'I'm still the same guy with the same defects,'" he said in an interview with the *Los Angeles Times*. "It's really weird."

DIKEMBE MUTOMBO

*Migrated from Democratic Republic
of the Congo in 1987*

★

He came to America to be a doctor, admitted to Georgetown on a USAID scholarship. But the university's basketball coach, who'd heard about the seven-foot-two Dikembe Mutombo's arrival on campus, had other plans.

According to his Georgetown teammates, Mutombo still had a lot to learn about the game. He had played basketball before but started late, joining the Congo's junior national squad as an older teenager. At college, Mutombo's academic interests took a turn toward the humanities—he interned at the World Bank and the Library of Congress and graduated with degrees in linguistics and diplomacy—and basketball became his career focus. Nicknamed "Mount Mutombo," he was drafted by the NBA's Denver Nuggets in the first round, and immediately turned the team's defensive play around, posting an average of 16.6 points, 12.3 rebounds, and three blocks per game in his all-star rookie season.

He became famous for his appendages: First for a taunting finger wag at an opponent after a block, like a parent scolding a naughty child, a move that so rankled competitors the NBA began counting it as a technical foul. Then for his long arms and rogue elbows, which injured famous competitors from Michael Jordan to LeBron James. Both made him recognizable to even informal fans, propelling the once staunchly American NBA to popularity across an increasingly global audience.

After retirement, Mutombo set his sights on medicine once more. He partnered with Georgetown to provide services for blind children from low-income families in Washington, D.C., and in 2007, his foundation opened the Biamba Marie Mutombo Hospital near his hometown in the Congo. The hospital, named for his late mother, is the first modern healthcare facility built there in nearly forty years.

AMERICAN CHAMPIONS

It's no secret that the American sports scene could never be the competitive field it is today without the participation of immigrants from around the globe. Twenty-seven percent of Major League Baseball players are born abroad, as were fifty Olympians on America's 2016 team in Rio de Janeiro.

FREDDY ADU (GHANA) Youngest athlete ever to sign a professional contract with a U.S. sports team (the D.C. United soccer club at age fourteen); youngest player to score a goal in Major League Soccer history.

NICHOLAS DELPOPOLO (MONTENEGRO) Winner of five bronze and one gold Pan-American Judo championship medals; competed for Team USA in the 2012 and 2016 Summer Olympics.

PATRICK EWING (JAMAICA) New York Knicks starting center; eleven-time NBA all-star; Olympic gold medalist and NBA and Olympic Hall of Fame inductee.

JULIETA GRANADA (PARAGUAY) First winner of the $1 million prize in women's golf at the ADT Championship in 2006; winner of the 2007 Women's World Cup of Golf; competed for Paraguay in the 2016 Summer Olympics.

ANDERSON LIM (BRUNEI) Became the first Bruneian to participate in an Olympic swimming event when he appeared in the 2012 Summer Olympics in London.

SOPHIA YOUNG-MALCOLM (ST. VINCENT AND THE GRENADINES)
Star of Baylor University's women's basketball team; drafted fourth overall to the San Antonio Stars; three-time WNBA all-star, 2006 to 2009.

EVGENI NABOKOV (KAZAKHSTAN) NHL goaltender, mainly for the San Jose Sharks; named NHL Rookie of the Year and won the Calder Memorial Trophy in 2001; on the NHL All-Star Team in 2008.

MARTINA NAVRATILOVA (CZECHOSLOVAKIA, NOW THE CZECH REPUBLIC) Considered the best female tennis player from 1975 to 2005 and one of the best of all time; winner of 18 Grand Slam titles, 9 Wimbledon titles, 31 major women's double titles, and 10 major mixed-doubles titles; one of three women ever to achieve a Grand Slam "boxed set"; the only player in history to have held the number one spot in the world in both singles and doubles for more than two hundred weeks.

KNUTE ROCKNE (NORWAY) Called "without question American football's most renowned coach" by the College Football Hall of Fame, he popularized the forward pass and began Notre Dame's football dynasty.

ARNOLD SCHWARZENEGGER (AUSTRIA) One of the greatest body-builders of all time; seven-time Mr. Olympia champion turned Terminator turned two-term governor of California.

VAI SIKAHEMA (TONGA) Running back and kickoff returner for the Arizona Cardinals, the Green Bay Packers, and the Philadelphia Eagles; the first Tongan ever to play in the NFL; now a Philadelphia sportscaster and reporter.

FRENCH MONTANA

Migrated from Morocco in 1996

★

French Montana is decidedly cavalier about the time he was shot in the head. He can't even remember the year, exactly, telling *Complex* in an interview that it was around 2003 or 2004. What happened? "I guess somebody had a hit out on me, and I came out the studio and got shot in the head," he said. You can almost picture the accompanying shrug. He's much more perturbed by the rumors that he got some kind of a settlement money for the injury, and that he used the funding to launch his career.

It makes sense that accusations of dependency on some unearned wellspring of cash might offend him. Montana, born Karim Kharbouch (he later fashioned his name after Tony Montana in *Scarface*), remembers little about the first twelve years of his life in Morocco, besides being poor. When he and his family arrived in the United States, the young teenager spoke Moroccan Darija and French, and picked up English on the South Bronx streets. After a few years, Montana's father would leave the family to return to Casablanca. His mother was pregnant with her third child.

By seventeen, Montana was the family's provider, doing whatever he could on and off the streets to earn money and selling DVDs as a battle rapper. Now a Grammy nominee and multimillionaire, he has a penchant for mink coats and exotic pets. But he is also known for his philanthropic work in East Africa; he is the first rapper to be named a Global Citizen Ambassador.

In 2012 he returned to Casablanca for the first time since he'd left. On the last day of his trip, he visited his father and proudly handed him ten thousand dollars.

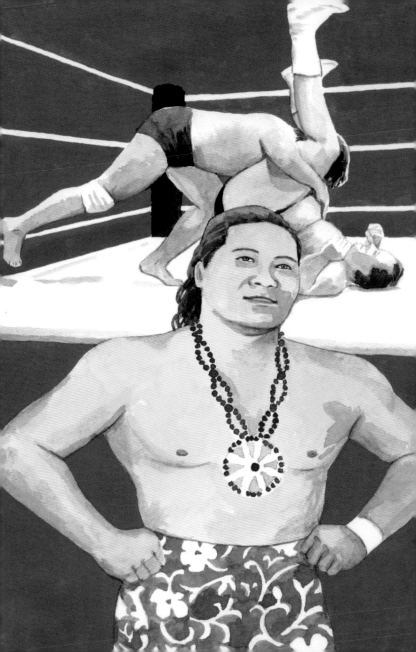

NEFF MAIAVA

Migrated from Samoa in 1926

★

Years before Stanislavski popularized method acting among theater students, Neff Maiava was already embodying the art of transforming oneself completely.

Born in Samoa and raised in Hawaii, Maiava was the first Samoan professional wrestler to catapult to mainstream fame; he is credited with paving the way for other Polynesian and Hawaiian sports entertainers, including wrestling tag team the Usos brothers; the "Flying Hawaiian" Peter Maivia (whose surname was changed to mimic Maiava's); and Maivia's grandson, superstar Dwayne "The Rock" Johnson.

When inhabiting his "wild brute" wrestling persona, Maiava performed fire dances, walked on nails, rubbed against the legs of female audience members, animal-like, and broke boards over his head. He wielded magic hair that "cut" his opponents when he swung it at them, and had a deadly signature "coconut headbutt." He even refused to speak English in public whenever he was outside Hawaii. While many of the antics catered to ethnic stereotypes, Maiava's showmanship fueled a rabid following: Fans became so invested in the story lines he crafted, one 1961 loss incited a riot that injured four police officers.

But Maiava came closest to revealing his true character in a performance at a National Wrestling Alliance match in which he fought a bear. After a few moments of circling, Maiava covered his chest in honey and lay down to let the bear lick it off, eventually flipping him over for a pin. It was this humor and sweetness that his children and friends say best represented the man they loved.

After he retired, he owned a tree-trimming business in Hawaii, and wrote songs and several children's books.

KEITH URBAN

*Migrated from New Zealand via
Australia in 1992*

Today's biggest U.S. country music star was born perhaps as far from the American heartland as you can get. Keith Urban's hometown of Whangarei, New Zealand, is a subtropical city that rests in the shadow of the volcano Mount Parihaka.

The son of a convenience store owner who was fascinated by American music, Urban was raised in Australia listening to Dolly Parton, Dire Straits, and Fleetwood Mac. He showed natural skills on the guitar and as a member of his local theater troupe, but it was his blond locks that would first open doors for him in Nashville; country star Alan Jackson told the *Australian Herald* that he hired Urban as a backup guitarist for his good looks.

Eventually, Urban's talent as a guitarist was recognized by musicians across genres, and the artists of his childhood would come to inform his revolutionary brand of country crossover music. Unafraid to use classic rock drumbeats and guitar riffs to accompany his country-style lyrics and twang, Urban strikes a careful balance between pop and country that appeals to listeners of both groups and has catapulted him to mainstream fame.

His willingness to take risks has earned him four Grammys, ten Country Music Awards, an American Music Award, and a Golden Globe nomination for Best Original Song. He's been a judge on *American Idol* and the Australian version of *The Voice*, and set sales records for his signature Home Shopping Network guitar line. All nine of his solo albums have gone platinum or multiplatinum, and he is a member of the Grand Ole Opry.

The life of a superstar keeps him busy, but Urban still finds time to spend below the equator. He and his wife, Nicole Kidman, along with their children, split their time between Los Angeles, New York City, Nashville, and Sydney.

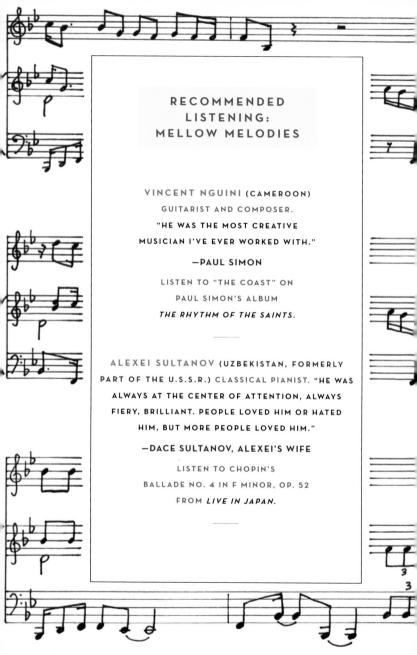

RECOMMENDED LISTENING: MELLOW MELODIES

VINCENT NGUINI (CAMEROON)
GUITARIST AND COMPOSER.
"HE WAS THE MOST CREATIVE
MUSICIAN I'VE EVER WORKED WITH."

—PAUL SIMON

LISTEN TO "THE COAST" ON
PAUL SIMON'S ALBUM
THE RHYTHM OF THE SAINTS.

———

ALEXEI SULTANOV (UZBEKISTAN, FORMERLY
PART OF THE U.S.S.R.) CLASSICAL PIANIST. "HE WAS
ALWAYS AT THE CENTER OF ATTENTION, ALWAYS
FIERY, BRILLIANT. PEOPLE LOVED HIM OR HATED
HIM, BUT MORE PEOPLE LOVED HIM."

—DACE SULTANOV, ALEXEI'S WIFE

LISTEN TO CHOPIN'S
BALLADE NO. 4 IN F MINOR, OP. 52
FROM *LIVE IN JAPAN.*

———

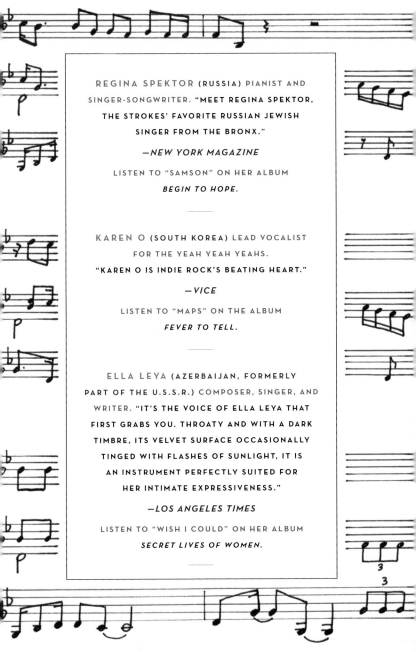

REGINA SPEKTOR (RUSSIA) PIANIST AND SINGER-SONGWRITER. "MEET REGINA SPEKTOR, THE STROKES' FAVORITE RUSSIAN JEWISH SINGER FROM THE BRONX."

—*NEW YORK MAGAZINE*

LISTEN TO "SAMSON" ON HER ALBUM *BEGIN TO HOPE.*

KAREN O (SOUTH KOREA) LEAD VOCALIST FOR THE YEAH YEAH YEAHS. "KAREN O IS INDIE ROCK'S BEATING HEART."

—*VICE*

LISTEN TO "MAPS" ON THE ALBUM *FEVER TO TELL.*

ELLA LEYA (AZERBAIJAN, FORMERLY PART OF THE U.S.S.R.) COMPOSER, SINGER, AND WRITER. "IT'S THE VOICE OF ELLA LEYA THAT FIRST GRABS YOU. THROATY AND WITH A DARK TIMBRE, ITS VELVET SURFACE OCCASIONALLY TINGED WITH FLASHES OF SUNLIGHT, IT IS AN INSTRUMENT PERFECTLY SUITED FOR HER INTIMATE EXPRESSIVENESS."

—*LOS ANGELES TIMES*

LISTEN TO "WISH I COULD" ON HER ALBUM *SECRET LIVES OF WOMEN.*

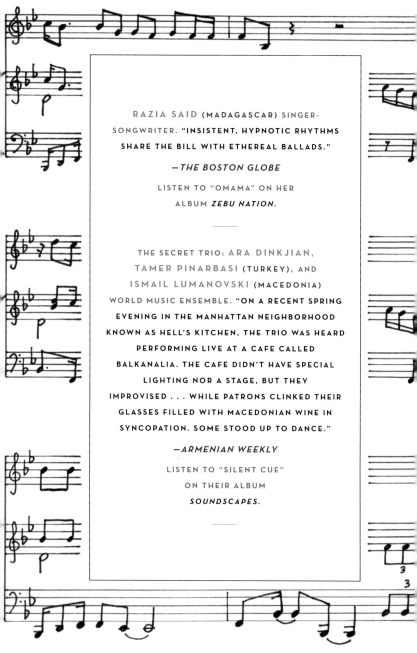

RAZIA SAID (MADAGASCAR) SINGER-SONGWRITER. "INSISTENT, HYPNOTIC RHYTHMS SHARE THE BILL WITH ETHEREAL BALLADS."

—*THE BOSTON GLOBE*

LISTEN TO "OMAMA" ON HER ALBUM *ZEBU NATION*.

THE SECRET TRIO: ARA DINKJIAN, TAMER PINARBASI (TURKEY), AND ISMAIL LUMANOVSKI (MACEDONIA) WORLD MUSIC ENSEMBLE. "ON A RECENT SPRING EVENING IN THE MANHATTAN NEIGHBORHOOD KNOWN AS HELL'S KITCHEN, THE TRIO WAS HEARD PERFORMING LIVE AT A CAFE CALLED BALKANALIA. THE CAFE DIDN'T HAVE SPECIAL LIGHTING NOR A STAGE, BUT THEY IMPROVISED . . . WHILE PATRONS CLINKED THEIR GLASSES FILLED WITH MACEDONIAN WINE IN SYNCOPATION. SOME STOOD UP TO DANCE."

—*ARMENIAN WEEKLY*

LISTEN TO "SILENT CUE" ON THEIR ALBUM *SOUNDSCAPES*.

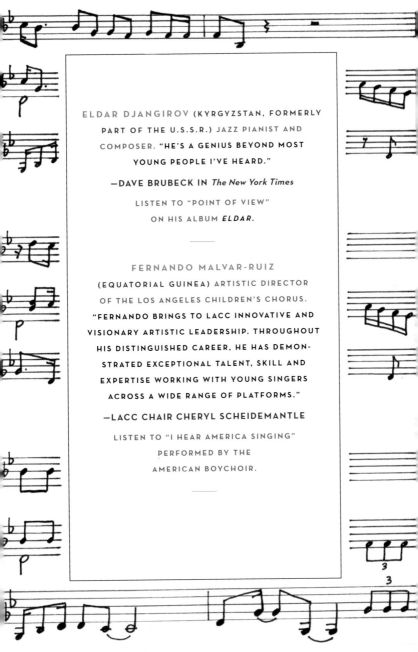

ELDAR DJANGIROV (KYRGYZSTAN, FORMERLY PART OF THE U.S.S.R.) JAZZ PIANIST AND COMPOSER. "HE'S A GENIUS BEYOND MOST YOUNG PEOPLE I'VE HEARD."

—DAVE BRUBECK IN *The New York Times*

LISTEN TO "POINT OF VIEW" ON HIS ALBUM *ELDAR*.

FERNANDO MALVAR-RUIZ (EQUATORIAL GUINEA) ARTISTIC DIRECTOR OF THE LOS ANGELES CHILDREN'S CHORUS. "FERNANDO BRINGS TO LACC INNOVATIVE AND VISIONARY ARTISTIC LEADERSHIP. THROUGHOUT HIS DISTINGUISHED CAREER, HE HAS DEMONSTRATED EXCEPTIONAL TALENT, SKILL AND EXPERTISE WORKING WITH YOUNG SINGERS ACROSS A WIDE RANGE OF PLATFORMS."

—LACC CHAIR CHERYL SCHEIDEMANTLE

LISTEN TO "I HEAR AMERICA SINGING" PERFORMED BY THE AMERICAN BOYCHOIR.

EXPLORERS

LHAKPA SHERPA

Migrated from Nepal circa 2002

★

The greatest ever female mountain climber works at a Connecticut 7-Eleven. Since her divorce from the Romanian-American mountaineer George Dijmarescu, with whom she climbed Everest five times, Lhakpa Sherpa works as a convenience store clerk and house cleaner to provide for her three children. Sherpa considers the jobs embarrassing but worth the sacrifice: As a child in Nepal, she had no access to formal education; her hard work in America means better opportunities for her kids.

And Sherpa is no stranger to difficult tasks; the female world record holder has summited Mount Everest nine times and was the first Nepali woman to summit the mountain and survive. At the time, she was pregnant with her second child. "It was not easy, but I managed all right," she told the BBC.

Born in the Himalayas as one of eleven children, Sherpa learned the mountains early, and worked as a mountaineering company's "kitchen boy" from the time she was a teen. Her siblings are also successful climbers, and she completed one of her summits with her brother and sister in 2003. Still, for many years Lhakpa Sherpa's accomplishments weren't recognized by the record books. The Sherpa people, one of Nepal's major ethnic groups, are often not credited for their mountaineering feats, unlike the foreigners who come to climb. This holds especially true for women, but now that Sherpa has caught the media's attention, she sees her expeditions as a way to tear down barriers. "I have been climbing mountains for women's empowerment," she said in an interview with *The Himalayan Times.*

Now, from her West Hartford apartment, Sherpa dreams of her tenth summit. "I'm still not tired," she told the BBC. "I want to climb Everest a few more times."

HUGO GERNSBACK

Migrated from Luxembourg in 1904

Before he created the genre of science fiction, he lived it. In the 1920s, while the rest of the world was still coming to terms with airplanes, Hugo Gernsback was fascinated by the questions of gravity and weightlessness that humans might encounter in space.

He coined the word *television* in English and was involved with some of the first primitive telecasts, which he sent out from his hotel-room-based WRNY local radio studio in 1928.

He had dreams of "teledoctoring"—video conferencing with a doctor—as a replacement for time-consuming house calls, and invented an early bone conduction hearing aid. His "teleyeglasses" were precursors to portable television and virtual reality goggles. One day, he prophesied, the world would get its news via "instant newspapers"—reading material transported to people's houses via electromagnetic waves.

All the while, Gernsback was a passionate writer and publisher of science fiction, a burgeoning genre for which he preferred the moniker *scientifiction*. He authored three novels and edited *Amazing Stories*, the first science fiction monthly magazine, among many other periodicals.

When the space race began in earnest between the United States and the Soviet Union, Gernsback was in his late seventies and thrilled to see space flight on the world stage. "My only reaction is this," he told *LIFE* magazine in 1963: "What took them so long?"

SPACE EXPLORERS

THEODORE VON KÁRMÁN (HUNGARY) One of the founders of the Jet Propulsion Laboratory, the leading U.S. center for the robotic exploration of the solar system, he is considered the top aerodynamic theorist of the twentieth century due to his advances in supersonic motion.

BILL PICKERING (NEW ZEALAND) The director of the Jet Propulsion Laboratory for twenty-two years, he oversaw many missions, including the launch of America's first satellite, Explorer 1, into orbit.

FAROUK EL-BAZ (EGYPT) This NASA scientist helped plan America's moon missions, including selecting Apollo landing sites and training astronauts in lunar observation, photography, and sample collection.

FRANKLIN CHANG-DÍAZ (OF COSTA RICAN, SPANISH, AND CHINESE DESCENT) A Hall of Fame astronaut, he tied the record for most space flights with seven NASA missions, one of which included out-of-spacecraft time to help build the International Space Station.

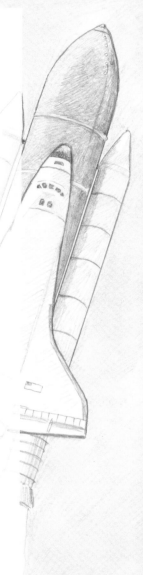

EREN AND FATIH OZMEN (TURKEY)
This couple founded the Sierra Nevada Corporation, a global high-tech aerospace company that contracts with the U.S. armed forces, NASA, and private spaceflight companies to build spacecraft, design deep-space habitats for humans, manage space transportation, and more. The company created the Dream Chaser spacecraft, which shuttles cargo to and from the International Space Station.

ANOUSHEH ANSARI (IRAN) The first self-funded woman to fly to the International Space Station, she was also the first Iranian in space.

KHALID AL-ALI (QATAR) Taking an early interest in science thanks to his parents—his mother was a nuclear physicist; his father, Qatar's first electrical engineer—he moved to the United States for university. He built drones and robots, and helped launch two spacecraft for NASA before founding his own artificial intelligence start-up, Senseta.

PEARL PRIMUS

Migrated from Trinidad and Tobago in 1921

While audiences would come to know her as America's preeminent performer and scholar of African dance, Pearl Primus herself saw things differently. Rather than being a master of one genre, she considered herself born of three mothers: "I have the mother where I was born, Trinidad, my Caribbean home; America, where I was educated, and primed, and sometimes deeply hurt . . . and then there's the mother Africa, who polished me."

Primus had long researched African and Afro-Caribbean movement, and is considered the first American choreographer to incorporate those styles into her own work. But she also performed and choreographed for Broadway shows, and trained with the New Dance Group and Martha Graham.

Her first solos were protest pieces set to blues music, most notably Billie Holiday's "Strange Fruit" and Langston Hughes's "The Negro Speaks of Rivers." Some of her solos were later recast to feature male dancers because it was so difficult to find female dancers who could execute Primus's famous five-foot-high leaps.

After an impressive performance at Fisk University, the university president learned that Primus had never been to Africa and offered her funding for a study tour of Ghana, Angola, Cameroon, Liberia, Senegal, and the Congo. For eighteen months, Primus participated in the daily lives of the communities she visited and meticulously documented their dances.

Upon her return to the States, her anthropological work upended assumptions that African dance was "primitive" or less complex than Western traditions. Her choreography had a profound impact on American modern dance, including the stylings of the world-famous Alvin Ailey American Dance Theater.

Primus used her fieldwork to earn a doctorate in anthropology at New York University in 1978. She was the university's first-ever student to fulfill her world-language requirement with dance.

THE VON TRAPP FAMILY

Migrated from Austria via Italy in 1938

★

The image of Julie Andrews as Maria, dancing before a background of the Swiss Alps and singing the titular ballad from *The Sound of Music*, is, according to the von Trapps, an iconic moment that never happened.

Before she was a nun, tutor, and eventually stepmother to the von Trapp children, the real-life Maria was an atheist and socialist, an orphan raised by relatives. Known for her terrible temper, she often screamed and threw things at the family. Her portrayal by Andrews, she told *The Washington Post*, was "too gentle—like girls out of Bryn Mawr." By contrast, Georg von Trapp—portrayed as cold in the film's first act—was actually quite tender and enjoyed his family's musical pursuits.

The von Trapp family—which consisted of ten children, not seven—*was* known for its classical and folk music skill, and *did* flee the Nazis on the pretense of a musical tour. But rather than a suitcase-laden hike through the mountains, they took a train—to Italy, not Switzerland. Georg, born in modern-day Croatia, which was then annexed by Italy, had Italian citizenship, and the family was able to procure safe passage to America.

After a six-month tour, the family had to leave the States to renew their tourist visas. According to Maria's memoir, they were detained at Ellis Island for several days upon their return because, when asked how long they intended to stay, she got so excited she blurted out, "Oh, I am so glad to be here—I never want to leave again!"

Eventually, the von Trapps settled in Vermont and ran a music camp when they weren't on tour. They received almost no monetary compensation for the movie based on their lives. "*The Sound of Music* simplifies everything," Johannes von Trapp told *The New York Times*. "I think perhaps reality is at the same time less glamorous, but more interesting than the myth."

RECOMMENDED READING FOR
CHILDREN AND YOUNG ADULTS

A is for Activist.
Abolitionist. Ally.
Actively Answering
A call to Action.
Are you an activist?

—INNOSANTO NAGARA,
A is for Activist

CHILDREN'S BOOKS

RENÉ COLATO LAÍNEZ **(EL SALVADOR)**
and Joe Cepeda, *From North to South*

INNOSANTO NAGARA **(INDONESIA)** *A is for Activist*

PATTI KIM **(SOUTH KOREA)** and Sonia Sánchez, *Here I Am*

EDWIDGE DANTICAT **(HAITI)** and Leslie Staub,
*Mama's Nightingale: A Story of Immigration
and Separation*

JO MORA

Migrated from Uruguay in the 1880s

★

The "Renaissance Man of the West," one of California's most prominent artists and cowboys, was raised in Perth Amboy, New Jersey. Rather than uncharted nature, terra-cotta and copper-smelting factories ruled the town. His father was a sculptor, and Jo Mora himself went to art schools in New York City and Boston before becoming a cartoonist for the *Boston Herald*.

An immigrant and East Coaster, it's this outsider's eye that allowed Mora to bring an anthropological note to his artwork. In 1903, he set out for California, curious about the West and interested in documenting Native American life. For several years after, he lived with the Hopi in Arizona, studying, taking part in, and chronicling their daily lives and community through photography and painting.

He'd carry this humanist perspective through the projects for which he would become most famous—a series of geographically accurate but subjective maps of the national parks and cities of the West, which always included a humor-infused look at a city's residents, and, in the case of his Carmel-by-the-Sea map, even a guide to the neighborhood's dogs.

At a time when cartography was wielded as a tool for establishing order and making sense of the unknown terrain of the American West, Mora's art reminded viewers of the most important component of the spirit of the place: its people.

YOKO ONO

Migrated from Japan via the United Kingdom in the 1970s

★

She was, for a time, the most hated woman in the world. In 1970, when Paul McCartney officially announced he was leaving the Beatles, fans and tabloids alike hurled often racist blame at Yoko Ono, who had been in a relationship with John Lennon since 1968 and had an undeniable influence on both his creative output and his politics.

McCartney and George Harrison have both since said she had nothing to do with the breakup; the band's problems long preceded her arrival. "I don't think you could've broken up four strong people like them," said Ono, according to *Rolling Stone*, "even if you tried." Still, her name became synonymous with the female interruption of male genius, with women ranging from Courtney Love to Jessica Simpson labeled "a Yoko" during periods of poor performance by their partners.

While Ono was often viewed as a hanger-on to Beatles' superstardom, she had a decade-long career as an artist under her belt before she even met Lennon. Her portfolio was stuffed with poetry, avant-garde exhibitions, performance art, short films, and music, and she was known for collaborating with the neo-Dadaist collective Fluxus. Alexandra Munroe, senior curator for Asian Art for the Solomon R. Guggenheim Museum and Foundation, noted that Ono was one of the first to use language within her art to invite audience participation and experimentation in the gallery context.

In recent years, retrospectives at the Museum of Modern Art, the Guggenheim, and the Musée d'art contemporain de Lyon have sought to rectify Ono's reputation, and in 2017, she received songwriting credit for "Imagine." Of course, Lennon revered her unmistakable talent far earlier, saying in a 1980 interview shortly before his murder: "I learned everything from her. . . . That's what people don't understand. She's the teacher and I'm the pupil."

NICK UT

Migrated from Vietnam via Japan in 1977

★

He became a photographer at age sixteen in South Vietnam, after his elder brother—an Associated Press photographer—was killed on the job. By twenty-one, he had taken a photo that would go on to win the 1973 Pulitzer Prize and the World Press Photo of the Year. "The Terror of War" captured a group of young children—one the fully nude nine-year-old Kim Phuc—fleeing from their napalm-bombed town. After he snapped the photo, he rushed the injured children to a hospital in Saigon.

"The Terror of War" was initially banned from the AP wire because it depicted frontal nudity, but several editors advocated for the image, and eventually it ran on the front page of *The New York Times*. President Nixon questioned its authenticity, suggesting it might've been "fixed," but most saw it as an all-too-real depiction of the war's human cost. The photo became a symbol and shorthand for the brutality of the American war in Vietnam.

Kim Phuc, who came to be known across the world as "Napalm Girl," was so severely burned she was not expected to survive her injuries. Ut visited her often over her fourteen-month hospital stay, until he was evacuated from the city, having himself been injured three times in the conflict. He went on to have a fifty-one-year career with the Associated Press, documenting everything from war to celebrity fanfare across the world.

Today, Ut lives with his wife in Los Angeles. He visits Kim Phuc—now in Canada—frequently, and speaks with her almost weekly by phone.

RECOMMENDED READING: GRAPHIC NOVELS, MEMOIRS, AND COMICS

Um...

Yes?

Comics are a gateway drug to literacy.

—ART SPIEGELMAN, AUTHOR OF *MAUS*

Palestine, JOE SACCO (MALTA)

Maus, ART SPIEGELMAN (BORN TO POLISH PARENTS IN SWEDEN)

STRAIGHTENER IS A I NEED MORE PRACTICE...

OW DO LOOK?

UALITY DISHES? NEVER

WE WATCHED UNTIL THEY DISAPPEARED FROM OUR EYES..

IT WAS THE LAST TIME EVER WE SAW THEM; BUT THAT WE COULDN'T KNOW.

HAS TO? YOU KNOW JACK ONLY MAKES THE DISHES DIRTIER WHEN SHE WASHES THEM... IS THIS DRESS AGE-APPROPRIATE?

YEAH, YOU'RE NOT THAT OLD..

The 99, NAIF AL-MUTAWA (KUWAIT)

El Iluminado, ILAN STAVANS (MEXICO) with Steve Sheinkin

Lena Finkle's Magic Barrel, ANYA ULINICH (RUSSIA)

The Best We Could Do, THI BUI (VIETNAM)

MARIO ANDRETTI

Migrated from Istria, Italy (now Croatia), in 1955

★

Before he'd even seen a car up close, Mario Andretti had fantasies of racing. His mother recalls him and his twin brother, as toddlers, using the lids of pots as steering wheels and shouting "vroom vroom" as they dashed around the kitchen.

Andretti and his family left their home on the Istrian peninsula during the post–World War II exodus, when the territory was annexed to Yugoslavia. At a refugee camp, the young twins raced in wooden derby cars and took turns playing with their uncle's motorcycle. As teenagers they got jobs at a garage so they could be closer to cars, and secretly joined a Formula Junior racing league against the wishes of their parents. "I don't remember as a kid wanting to do or be anything else but drive something," Andretti told *ESPN*.

When they arrived in Pennsylvania, the family had only $125 and didn't speak English, but Andretti and his brother were thrilled to find a half-mile dirt track nearby. They saved up their money to fix an old car, which they took turns racing. The two were evenly matched, but it was Mario, the more cautious of the two, who'd go on to achieve international success; his brother was severely injured in an early crash. Andretti forged a driver's license to enter bigger competitions, eventually becoming one of the most famous race car drivers in the world.

Now his name is synonymous with speed. Successful in both NASCAR and Formula One formats, he's the only driver ever to have won the Daytona 500, the Indianapolis 500, and the Formula One World Championship. "If you wait," Andretti said in his autobiography, "all that happens is you get older."

M. NIGHT SHYAMALAN

Migrated from India in 1970

★

M. Night Shyamalan sees dead people. Sometimes, he hears their voices, too. A victim of an icy drowning in childhood, he lay dead for thirty minutes before he was revived, leaving him with a lasting connection to the spirit realm.

It seems a plausible origin story for a writer and director hailed for a time as the next Hitchcock. But the tale is a tall one, part of a faux documentary made by the Sci-Fi Channel to stir up excitement about *The Village*, Shyamalan's forthcoming movie at the time. The truth is perhaps more interesting.

Shyamalan was born in India and was a baby when his family migrated to an affluent Philadelphia suburb. He was raised Hindu, but attended Catholic schools. His parents, both doctors, had hoped he would follow in their footsteps. Rather than some freak accident, it was a childhood spent among these varied worldviews that created the signature blend of the supernatural, spiritual, and sci-fi in Shyamalan's films.

He made films during and shortly after his time as an NYU film student; the 1999 smash hit *The Sixth Sense* was his first major motion picture. The thriller, which Shyamalan wrote and directed, frightened and delighted audiences across the nation and was an unprecedented success. The film grossed nearly $673 million worldwide, and Shyamalan was one of the youngest people ever to be nominated for an Academy Award for Best Director.

Now for the twist ending: Shyamalan's third-highest-grossing movie, behind *The Sixth Sense* and *Signs*? The adaptation of E. B. White's classic novel *Stuart Little*. Shyamalan co-wrote the screenplay for the children's hit, which was directed by Rob Minkoff and released in the same year as *The Sixth Sense*.

FROM WRITER / DIRECTOR
M. NIGHT SHYAMALAN

The 1939 comedy *Ninotchka,* in which normally stoic beauty GRETA GARBO (SWEDEN) showed off her comic touch; the advertising campaign touted, "Garbo laughs!"

ALFRED HITCHCOCK'S (UNITED KINGDOM) *Vertigo,* 1958, the British Film Institute's 2012 pick for best film ever made

One of film's most beloved romantic comedies, *Some Like It Hot,* 1959, written, produced, and directed by BILLY WILDER (AUSTRIA)

Horror staple *The Texas Chain Saw Massacre,* 1974, featuring GUNNAR HANSEN (ICELAND) as the slasher Leatherface

Family favorites *The Muppet Show,* 1976–1981, and *The Muppet Movie,* 1979, featuring EREN OZKER (TURKEY), the only full-time female Muppeteer at the time

NBC's twenty-two-time Emmy-winning series *ER,* featuring C.C.H. POUNDER (GUYANA) as Dr. Angela Hicks

GoldenEye, 1995, starring PIERCE BROSNAN (IRELAND) as Bond . . . James Bond

LUCY LAWLESS (NEW ZEALAND) as the war-cry-screaming star of the cult-classic TV series *Xena: Warrior Princess,* 1995–2001

Rush Hour, 1998, starring international martial arts superstar JACKIE CHAN (CHINA)

The family megahit *Ice Age*, 2002, with JOHN LEGUIZAMO (COLOMBIA) as Sid the Sloth

Frida, 2002, starring SALMA HAYEK (MEXICO) as Frida Kahlo

Monster, 2003, starring the nearly unrecognizable Academy Award winner CHARLIZE THERON (SOUTH AFRICA)

ABC's Emmy-winning television series *Lost*, 2004–10, with MIRA FURLAN (CROATIA)

Martin Scorsese's *The Aviator*, 2004, featuring two-time Academy Award winner CATE BLANCHETT (AUSTRALIA) as Academy Award winner Katharine Hepburn

Brokeback Mountain, 2005, depicting the lifelong love between two cowboys, directed by Academy Award winner ANG LEE (TAIWAN)

The haunting Spanish-language drama *Volver*, 2006, starring Academy Award winner PENÉLOPE CRUZ (SPAIN)

Longtime children's classic television series *Sesame Street*, featuring NITYA VIDYASAGAR (ETHNICALLY INDIAN, BORN IN OMAN) as Leela from 2008 to 2016

The Coen Brothers' *Inside Llewyn Davis*, 2013, starring Golden Globe winner OSCAR ISAAC (GUATEMALA)

PHILLIP BUCK

Migrated from North Korea via South Korea in 1982

★

The Reverend Phillip Buck was nearly seventy in 2005 when, after years of close calls, the Chinese authorities finally captured him. He spent fifteen months in prison before the U.S. Embassy intervened. Buck, an evangelical pastor, said he was simply on a mission to care for people, but Chinese and North Korean authorities viewed his actions as overtly political: In his decades-long career, he had aided countless refugees in their escape from North Korea.

Since the start of Kim Jong-il's repressive regime, many North Korean refugees have fled to China, where they have no legal path to citizenship. China's close political ties to North Korea mean a strict policy of deportation back to North Korea, where refugees are likely to face forced labor or the death penalty. Because of this, North Korean refugees in China have few resources and are vulnerable to starvation, forced marriage, and human trafficking.

Buck, born John Yoon, was separated from his family during the Korean War and was cared for in a South Korean orphanage. He studied theology and migrated to Seattle in 1982, but dedicated his life to supporting North Korean refugees. This was dangerous work; he officially changed his name to Phillip Buck in 2002 after an informant infiltrated his safe houses, nearly leading to his arrest. In addition to feeding and sheltering refugees, Buck personally guided more than two hundred individuals to safe passage to South Korea, where they could request asylum. These serpentine journeys often covered ten thousand miles by land and water to avoid detection.

Though he was deported and banned from China, Buck still devotes himself to the safety of North Korean refugees, offering financial and organizational support to those on the ground. His arrest had only emboldened him. "After I was released from prison," Buck told PBS, "I had no fear at all. I could speak with power."

For countries with small diasporas, or those whose immigrant populations—as a result of colonialism and remaining spheres of colonial influence—tend to concentrate in European countries or Australia rather than the United States, a nation's ambassador becomes an essential carrier of culture to those of us who might otherwise have limited exposure to the rich histories, languages, and traditions of these places. Frequently stationed in New York City for years at a time, ambassadors also work to support philanthropic and educational causes in their home-away-from-home local communities.

JULI MINOVES (ANDORRA) Having served terms as ambassador to the United States, the United Kingdom, Canada, Spain, Switzerland, Finland, and the United Nations, he now teaches political science in Southern California.

SERGE MOMBOULI (REPUBLIC OF CONGO) Ambassador to the United States since 2001, he uses his business acumen to strengthen U.S.-Congo relations in the public and private sectors. He also studied innovation for economic development as a student in Harvard's executive education program.

CELESTINO MIGLIORE (HOLY SEE) Serving as the permanent observer of the Holy See to the United Nations from 2003 to 2010, Archbishop Migliore couldn't vote in the general assembly, but often offered insight from his spot at the epicenter of the Catholic Church. He's best known for his five-step plan for nuclear disarmament and adherence to the United Nations' nonproliferation treaties; he also supported stricter oversight for non-weapons-related nuclear energy.

MARLENE MOSES (NAURU) Representative to the United Nations since 2005, she was involved in discussions on regulation of tuna fishing and whaling in Nauruan territorial waters. She continues to raise awareness about the impact of the industrialized nations on climate and rising sea levels.

MOHAMED TOIHIRI (COMOROS) Previously a French lecturer at the University of Michigan, he served as Comoros's representative to the United Nations from 2007 to 2012. He's also credited as the country's first published author.

RONALD JUMEAU (SEYCHELLES) From 2007 to 2012, he served as the ambassador to the United States and the United Nations, and has since taken up international activism to raise awareness about the dangers for developing island nations already suffering from the effects of climate change.

HOUDA NONOO (BAHRAIN) Ambassador to the United States from 2008 to 2013, she was the first female ambassador from Bahrain to the United States, and the first Jewish ambassador of any Arabic Middle Eastern nation. During her tenure, she changed iftar meals at the embassy from all-male to mixed-gender gatherings, and introduced interfaith events that incorporated the local community.

CARLOS FILOMENO AGOSTINHO DAS NEVES (SÃO TOMÉ AND PRÍNCIPE) Previously an ambassador to Spain and Portugal, he became the representative to the United Nations in 2012, a position he still holds. He was also the ambassador to the United States from 2013 to 2017. At home in São Tomé and Príncipe, he helps field and negotiate international entities' offshore petroleum-drilling requests.

MAGUY MACCARIO DOYLE (MONACO) The current ambassador to the United States and Canada, she has long served on the advisory board for St. Jude's Children's Research Hospital, and is the vice president of the U.S. chapter of the Prince Albert II of Monaco Foundation, which seeks to promote environmental sustainability initiatives.

TEBURORO TITO (KIRIBATI) A former teacher, he was elected president of Kiribati three times, and oversaw the country's entry into the United Nations. He then became ambassador to the United States and the United Nations, where he continues to speak out about the dangers of climate change for the South Pacific.

ODO TEVI (VANUATU) With a background in economics, having previously served at the World Bank and the International Monetary Fund, he's been Vanuatu's representative to the United Nations since 2016, and has completed executive training at Harvard and Columbia University.

THINKERS

MARYAM MIRZAKHANI

Migrated from Iran circa 2000

She wanted to be a writer.

As a child in Tehran, Maryam Mirzakhani poured herself into her studies with the goal of authoring books. But in high school, after winning several international mathematics competitions, she found herself drawn instead to that field, which she sometimes likened to detective work.

As a PhD student at Harvard, she called herself a slow mathematician, working methodically on problems for hours on end. Her meticulous efforts paid off: Mirzakhani is the first and only woman and Iranian to win the Fields Medal, mathematics' most prestigious award. But at the time of her 2014 win, she was already a year into her battle with breast cancer. She died in 2017, at the age of forty.

Mirzakhani's work examined intersections of dynamics and geometry, studying the symmetry and trajectory of curved surfaces. Some of her discoveries have already been applied in quantum field theory, physics, and cryptology, but colleagues are quick to point out that her work is likely ahead of its time, containing concrete applications that are yet to be discovered.

If not a writer in the end, Mirzakhani was still a creator of worlds unseen by others; she often drew complex shapes on large sheets of paper spread out before her, work her young daughter would call "painting." The solutions she teased out will remain an integral part of the mathematical narrative for years to come.

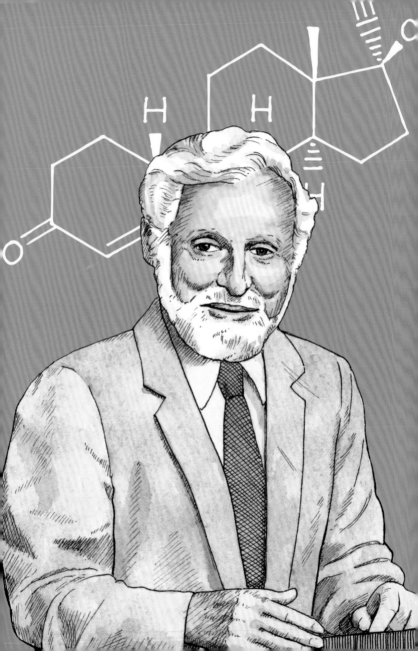

CARL DJERASSI

Of Bulgarian descent; migrated via Austria in 1939

★

He was sixteen when he left for America, broke and fleeing the Nazis. When he and his mother arrived in New York City, a cab driver promptly stole their last twenty dollars. With no other prospects, Carl Djerassi did the only thing he could think of: He wrote to Eleanor Roosevelt. He asked for a place at American University; she gave him a scholarship. A little more than a decade later his scientific research would forever change the face of contraception and American sexual politics.

Nicknamed the "father of the pill," Djerassi himself disliked the label. He would've preferred to have been called the pill's mother, but was also adamant that, like the creation and birth of a child, the project required more than one person. Scientists had already known that upping hormone levels could block ovulation, but producing those hormones synthetically was difficult. Djerassi was part of a team that had been researching fertility, menstrual disorders, and cervical cancer when they successfully synthesized a progestin hormone that would become the central ingredient in modern contraceptives.

The social, economic, and sexual ramifications of widely available and effective oral birth control were something Djerassi would explore in depth through scientific writing for the rest of his life. But in his later years, the polymath would shift his focus to the creative arts. "I feel like I'd like to lead one more life," he said. "I'd like to leave a cultural imprint on society rather than just a technological benefit."

He'd go on to write poetry, stage plays, and several novels, often integrating scientific elements into his fictional worlds. He also established an artists' colony in honor of his late daughter, Pamela, a poet and a painter. Today, Djerassi's 583-acre California property is the largest free artist residency in the western United States.

ALBERT EINSTEIN

Migrated from Germany in 1933

★

His family called him *der depperte*—"the dopey one." His parents, worried about his slow development, took him to the doctor; even after his speech caught up with his peers', he thought in pictures rather than words. At school, his contempt for authority angered some of his teachers, inspiring one to make the infamous prediction that he would never amount to anything.

But despite apocryphal stories to the contrary, Albert Einstein never failed math. His natural aptitude for science and mathematics was evident early on: At age twelve he taught himself geometry over summer vacation, finding a new way to prove the Pythagorean theorem; by fifteen he had command over differential and integral calculus.

His theory of special relativity, expressed by the formula $E = mc^2$, is the most famous equation in the world. Arguably his law of photoelectric effect—the idea that light behaves as both a wave and a particle—is even more impressive, with applications in solar cells, fiber optics, and telecommunications.

Einstein's politics were as progressive as his physics. When he fled Germany, it was with a Nazi bounty on his head, listed as an enemy of the state "not yet hanged." In America, conservative groups protested his visa due to his leftist leanings. He was an ardent voice against Hitler, fascism, and nationalism, a strong proponent of nuclear disarmament and a unified world government, and was even offered the presidency of Israel after World War II.

A far cry from his childhood nickname, *Einstein* would come to be a synonym for genius. Einstein, though, didn't consider himself exceptional, crediting his childhood antiauthoritarian streak with giving him the means to see beyond the conventional understanding of the universe. "I have no special talents," he told his biographer. "I am only passionately curious."

THE MANHATTAN PROJECT

July 16, 1945, 5:29 A.M.: A fiery plume rises above the desert in New Mexico, bright orange against the dark morning sky. As the flames burgeon outward, they form the soon-to-be-iconic mushroom cloud, 7.5 miles tall, a shape that will become synonymous with mass destruction. The source of the blast is the Gadget, an implosion-type weapon with a plutonium core, dropped from a one-hundred-foot tower. Four hundred and twenty-five people were present to bear witness to the Trinity Test, the world's first detonation of a nuclear weapon.

Beginning as an army initiative, several projects combined in 1939 to form what we know today as the Manhattan Project. It eventually employed 130,000 people across more than thirty laboratory and testing sites in the United States, Canada, and the United Kingdom, and cost today's equivalent of $32 billion. The research produced the world's first nuclear weapons, two of which were used on the Japanese cities Hiroshima and Nagasaki in August 1945. Estimates place the combined casualties of the bombs at about 225,000 people.

The Manhattan Project and bombing of Japan ushered in the atomic age, which would radically transform the bounds of international relations and global conflict. Lead scientists for the project hailed from around the world, and many were refugees from Nazi-occupied Europe. Some had known little about how their work would be used in a larger weapons context, and spent the remainder of their lives advocating for nuclear energy regulation, disarmament, and pacifism.

A partial list of project scientists:

HANS BETHE (GERMANY)

ROSE BETHE (GERMANY)

FELIX BLOCH (SWITZERLAND)

NIELS BOHR (DENMARK, TEMPORARY REFUGEE WORKER)

HANS COURANT (GERMANY)

ENRICO FERMI (ITALY)

JAMES FRANCK (GERMANY)

GERHART FRIEDLANDER (GERMANY)

OTTO FRISCH (AUSTRIA, TEMPORARY REFUGEE WORKER)

KLAUS FUCHS (GERMANY, TEMPORARY WORKER AND SOVIET SPY)

SAMUEL GOUDSMIT (NETHERLANDS)

LILLI HORNING (CZECHOSLOVAKIA, NOW THE CZECH REPUBLIC)

ROLF LANDSHOFF (GERMANY)

IRENE LAVIOLETTE (AMERICAN AND GREEK DUAL RESIDENT)

PETER LAX (HUNGARY)

RUDOLF PEIERLS (GERMANY / UNITED KINGDOM,
ON TEMPORARY ASSIGNMENT)

ISIDOR RABI (POLAND)

EUGENE RABINOWITCH (RUSSIA)

CHAIM RICHMAN (POLAND)

BRUNO ROSSI (ITALY)`

EMILIO SEGRÈ (ITALY)

JOHN SHACTER (AUSTRIA)

LEO SZILARD (HUNGARY)

EDWARD TELLER (HUNGARY)

AUGUSTA "MICI" TELLER (HUNGARY)

STANISŁAW ULAM (POLISH; BORN IN
AUSTRIA-HUNGARY, NOW UKRAINE)

JOHN VON NEUMANN (HUNGARY)

VICTOR WEISSKOPF (AUSTRIA)

EUGENE WIGNER (HUNGARY)

MARIA GOEPPERT MAYER (GERMAN; BORN IN
PRUSSIA, NOW POLAND)

CHIEN-SHIUNG WU (CHINA)

KAHLIL GIBRAN

*Migrated from Lebanon (then part of
the Ottoman Empire) in 1895*

★

Kahlil Gibran was born poor, one of four siblings mired in their father's gambling debts with no access to formal schooling. As a young boy he was drawn to nature and prone to wandering. By some biographical accounts he fell off a cliff at age ten, dislocating his shoulder. To stabilize it, his family tied his arm to a cross-shaped support for forty days as a reminder of Christ's forty days in the wilderness. Though the story was never confirmed, the image of a young Gibran tied to a cross foreshadows his future place within the canon of spiritual texts.

When he was twelve, his father was jailed, and his mother sought a new life for the family in America, where Gibran had access to education for the first time and became interested in writing and art. Several artists were taken with his sketches and made him their mentee. Over his lifetime Gibran completed more than seven hundred paintings, and would always consider himself a painter rather than a poet.

Gibran produced several volumes of poetry in Arabic and English before his most famed work, a book of prose poems called *The Prophet*, was published in 1923. The collection offered readers an abundance of spiritual, but nondenominational, wisdom. The book was an instant success and remains one of the most widely quoted texts today, a staple at weddings, funerals, and on the inspirational social media circuit.

Though *The Prophet* was written in English, Gibran is celebrated in the Arabic tradition as a modernist writer and a revolutionary who separated spirituality and religion in his work. Meanwhile, American critics were quick to dismiss his writing as saccharine, resisting his canonization despite his enduring popularity. Gibran remains the third-best-selling poet in the world today, after Shakespeare and Chinese philosopher Lao-tzu.

ELISABETH KÜBLER-ROSS

Migrated from Switzerland in 1958

★

Elisabeth Kübler-Ross was no stranger to death. Born in 1926, she was one of triplets and weighed only two pounds. At age five, battling pneumonia, she watched her hospital roommate die.

She wanted to be a doctor, but her father forbade it, suggesting she become a secretary. Instead she left home as a teen and volunteered to care for World War II refugees. On one visit to the Polish concentration camp Majdanek, Kübler-Ross was struck by the hundreds of butterflies victims had carved into the walls; the images would shape her thinking about life and death for years to come.

Kübler-Ross went on to study medicine in Zurich but was disheartened by the lack of training aspiring doctors received about the experience of dying. When she migrated to the United States, she chose a specialization in psychiatry. In 1969, she released her most famous work, *On Death and Dying*, which advocated for hospice care and outlined the five stages of grief for the terminally ill. At a time when talk of death was largely repressed, Kübler-Ross's work had a transformative impact on the field of medicine. The five stages of grief are still used today to understand the emotions of both patients and survivors.

In the 1980s, Kübler-Ross turned her attention to the AIDS crisis, attempting to open a hospice center for children with AIDS on her Virginia farm. The community launched a series of attacks against the project, eventually burning down her home.

But with all her life's work focused on death, Kübler-Ross never lost sight of how best to keep living. "I was educated in line with the basic premise: work work work," she once wrote. "This is utterly wrong. Half working, half dancing—that is the right mixture."

JAIME ESCALANTE

Migrated from Bolivia in 1963

★

Two years into his posting at Garfield High School in East Los Angeles, the man who would become America's most famous math teacher tried to quit.

When Jaime Escalante started at Garfield in 1974, the school was at a low point: Its accreditation had been threatened, gang turf wars raged, and teachers expected little of their "troubled" students. Escalante was assigned to teach basic math, the equivalent of what a fifth grader would study in Bolivia.

Discouraged, Escalante called the computer-testing company for which he'd previously worked to ask for his job back, but ultimately decided against leaving. Instead of sinking with the school's low expectations, Escalante began teaching algebra to his basic math students. By 1978, he was running the school's first Advanced Placement (AP) calculus class.

Escalante taught his students—mostly Latino, and mostly the children of undocumented workers—that Mayans had invented the concept of zero, so they carried math in their blood. He played "We Will Rock You" to warm up the class, wore funny hats, and threw a velvet pillow at those who zoned out. He encouraged the students to set a goal they'd been taught wasn't for them: college.

At the peak of the program's success, hundreds of students were passing the AP calculus exam, Garfield was offering sixteen other AP courses, and Hollywood immortalized Escalante in the film *Stand and Deliver*. Though the program waned when he retired, its aftereffects would radiate out into the community for years to come. "To this day he remains the single most influential person in my life," former student Angel Navarro, now an attorney, told the *Los Angeles Times* after Escalante's death. "What I learned during the ten months in his classroom twenty-eight years ago continues to be the basis of everything that I do."

AMERICAN EDUCATED

America prides itself on its higher education system, and one of the attributes that makes it so valuable is the opportunity for all students to be exposed to new ideas, cultures, and people. Though most of them are not permanent immigrants, the following individuals all boast impressive academic achievement at top American schools, and have subsequently gone on to use their education to support their home countries.

HAGE GEINGOB (NAMIBIA, FORMERLY SOUTH-WEST AFRICA) Arriving in the States to attend college, he received his bachelor's degree from Fordham University and his master's in international relations from The New School before returning home to become the first prime minister of Namibia.

MOHAMMED WAHEED HASSAN (MALDIVES) Originally an English teacher, he was awarded a scholarship to Stanford, where he studied education planning. Afterward, he returned home to work for the Ministry of Education as well as the United Nations and UNESCO; he eventually became the nation's fifth president. He is also notable for being the first person to appear on Maldivian television.

JOSÉ RAMOS-HORTA (TIMOR-LESTE) The first prime minister, and later president, of Timor-Leste, he received his master's degree in peace studies at Antioch College in the quiet town of Yellow Springs, Ohio. He also completed postgraduate work at Columbia University.

MOHAMMED MAHFOODH AL ARDHI (OMAN) After completing fighter pilot training during his Omani military service, he studied at the National Defense University in Washington, D.C., and later earned a master's in public administration at Harvard's Kennedy School. He returned to Oman to head up the air force for more than a decade, and later became chairman of the National Bank of Oman.

EVAN JEREMY PAKI (PAPUA NEW GUINEA) A Fulbright scholar, he earned a law degree from Harvard University before becoming Papua New Guinea's ambassador to the United States, Canada, and Mexico.

JAMAL KHASHOGGI (SAUDI ARABIA) A student of business administration at Indiana State University, he was originally an Islamist who, over the years, developed more progressive ideas on the separation of church and state, antisectarianism, and gender equality in the Middle East—views that caused him to flee Saudi Arabia in 2017. He became a columnist for *The Washington Post* before his assassination in 2018.

SUSANA EDJANG (EQUATORIAL GUINEA) A 2014 Yale World Fellow, she specializes in global health and has spearheaded various UN and NGO initiatives on international health, development, and climate change issues. She's currently Equatorial Guinea's minister counselor for Security Council Affairs at the United Nations.

ISHMAEL BEAH

Migrated from Sierra Leone in 1998

★

Over the course of a bloody civil war that lasted more than a decade, war crimes in Sierra Leone were often too many to count. One under-recognized atrocity committed by both the Sierra Leonean government forces and the Revolutionary United Front was the kidnapping and conscription of child soldiers. By 1999, government forces admitted that one-fifth of their army was underage, while estimates put the RUF soldiers at 50 percent children, some as young as seven.

Ishmael Beah was captured by government forces after his village was destroyed and his family murdered by RUF forces. At twelve years old, Beah was eager to interpret his new army's missions as vengeance for his family members' deaths. During his three-year period as a soldier, he killed more people than he could count.

Afterward, fighting off drug withdrawal and trauma in a Freetown rehabilitation center, Beah resented his return to powerless civilian status. A Run-DMC cassette tape served as a fulcrum for his healing. The music reminded him of his life before the war; he'd had a happy childhood surrounded by a strong community and enjoyed playing soccer and reading Shakespeare. Though he was only fifteen, he could never be a child again. He could, though, decide to move forward, in his own life and as an advocate for others. In 2007, he became a UNICEF spokesperson for children affected by war.

Beah would publish a harrowing, bestselling account of his time as a soldier, *A Long Way Gone*, but it's his second book, a work of fiction called *Radiance of Tomorrow*, that seems to hold the key to his life's philosophy: "We must live in the radiance of tomorrow, as our ancestors have suggested in their tales. For what is yet to come tomorrow has possibilities. . . . That will be our strength. That has always been our strength."

EDWARD SAID

Migrated from Palestine via Egypt in 1951

★

Before he made the concept of "otherness" a staple in literary and critical theory, he felt it himself. Born in Palestine, Edward Said lived in Lebanon and Egypt and arrived in the United States as a teenager to attend boarding school. An Arabic Christian, he frequently found himself feeling alienated. He titled his memoir *Out of Place*.

"It is geography," he wrote, "especially in the displaced form of departures, arrivals, farewells, exile, nostalgia, homesickness, belonging, and travel itself—that is at the core of my memories of those early years."

When he was a child, Palestine was a British-occupied territory; by the time he'd departed, it was the site of a dangerous border dispute with the freshly established state of Israel. The displacement Said felt fueled him to write his most famous work, *Orientalism*, which shed light on the way the West portrayed and understood other cultures, particularly Middle Eastern and Islamic ones, through stereotypes. The text would become foundational in postcolonial studies, a field of academic study of which he is now considered a founder. In the political sphere, Said advocated tirelessly for the rights of Palestinian civilians, a practice that earned him an FBI file hundreds of pages long.

Since his death in 2003, much has been written about his body of work, but the Palestinian poet Mahmoud Darwish best captures the essence of Said himself in a poem Darwish wrote to bid him farewell:

> *He says: I am from there, I am from here,*
> *but I am neither there nor here.*
> *I have two names which meet and part . . .*
> *I have two languages, but I have long forgotten*
> *which is the language of my dreams.*

RECOMMENDED READING:
NONFICTION AND MEMOIRS

*From the errors of
other nations,
let us learn wisdom.*

—THOMAS PAINE, *Common Sense*

THOMAS PAINE (UNITED KINGDOM)
Common Sense, 1776

HANNAH ARENDT (GERMANY)
The Origins of Totalitarianism, 1951

JAMAICA KINCAID
(ANTIGUA AND BARBUDA)
A Small Place, 1988

LUC SANTE (BELGIUM)
*Low Life: Lures and Snares of
Old New York,* 1991

CRAIG FERGUSON (UNITED KINGDOM)
American on Purpose: The Impossible Adventures of an Unlikely Patriot, 2009

WILLIAM KAMKWAMBA (MALAWI)
The Boy Who Harnessed the Wind, 2009

MASHA GESSEN (RUSSIA)
*The Man Without a Face:
The Unlikely Rise of Vladimir Putin,* 2012

ELIZABETH NUNEZ (TRINIDAD AND TOBAGO)
Not for Everyday Use, 2014

GARY SHTEYNGART (RUSSIA)
Little Failure, 2014

PADMA LAKSHMI (INDIA)
Love, Loss and What We Ate, 2016

FAN NOLI

Migrated from an ethnically Albanian village of Eastern Thrace (then part of the Ottoman Empire) in 1932

★

In March 1927, Harvard's student newspaper ran a short piece on the political turmoil roiling early-twentieth-century Albania, and the alum at its center: "Albania is a country of grim politics, sudden tribal uprisings, secret murders, and foreign intrigues. No man was [ever] better suited to such an environment than Fan Noli."

Noli was an idealist foremost. He graduated from Harvard in 1912, and set to work supporting Albanian language and culture through the arts and humanities. He wrote poetry and criticism; translated Shakespeare, Cervantes, and Poe; and helped standardize a unified Albanian language from regional dialects. He campaigned for his birth country's entry into the League of Nations to solidify its international recognition as an independent nation.

By 1924, he'd returned to Albania and delivered a passionate speech credited with inciting the June Revolution's peasant insurgency, which captured the capital and saw former leader Ahmed Bey Zogu expelled from the country. Noli was named prime minister and sought to establish a constitution-based government and modernize the agrarian economy.

His government was overthrown by Zogu's Yugoslav-backed army just months later, and Noli returned to the United States in exile. Instead of sinking into obscurity, the fifty-year-old Noli went back to school, studying at the New England Conservatory of Music, and earning a PhD from Boston University. He continued to teach, write, and translate literary masterpieces into Albanian and English, his belief in intellectual curiosity and the power of the written word never wavering.

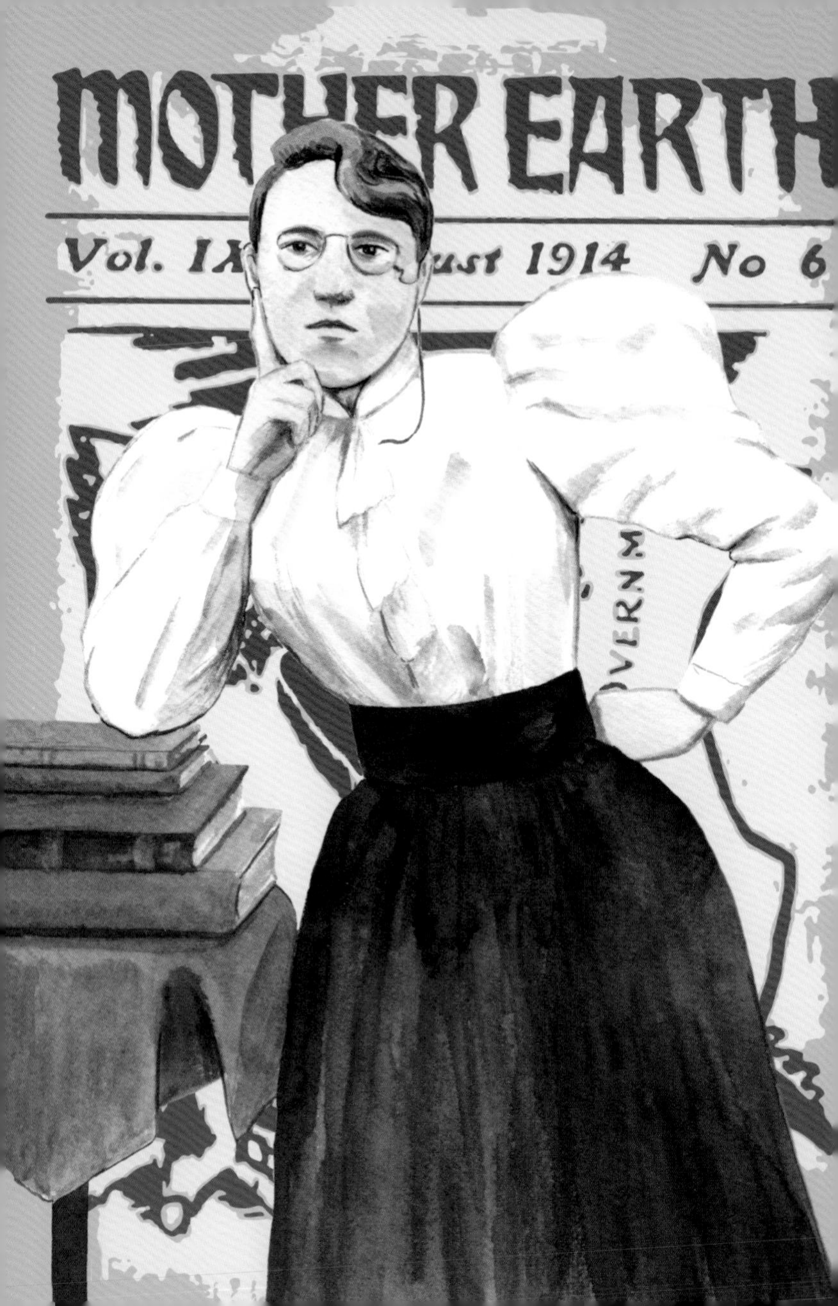
MOTHER EARTH
Vol. IX
ust 1914
No 6
OVERNM

EMMA GOLDMAN

Migrated from Lithuania in 1885

★

"It is too bad that we no longer live in the times when witches were burned at the stake or tortured to drive the evil spirit out of them. For, indeed, Emma Goldman is a witch! True, she does not eat little children, but she does many worse things."

Thus begins the opening of Goldman's own essay "What I Believe," in which she mocked the hysteria about her radical politics and laid out her foundational beliefs. "I want freedom, the right to self-expression, everybody's right to beautiful, radiant things," Goldman wrote later in her autobiography. But what radiant things might be worse, in the eyes of her detractors, than eating children? Unconstrained freedom of speech, press, and expression; workers' and union rights; anti-militarism; and women's equality, sexual freedom, and access to birth control.

Goldman's belief that capitalism oppressed the working man made her no friends in places of power. Her fiery speeches and her publication of the anarchist magazine *Mother Earth*, combined with her anti-draft activism as the United States was on the brink of entering World War I, landed her in federal prison. By then, J. Edgar Hoover had labeled Goldman and her lover, Alexander Berkman, "beyond doubt, two of the most dangerous anarchists in this country." Allowing them to return to their New York City–based community, he said, would, "do undue harm." When Goldman was released, she, along wth several hundred other "radical aliens," were deported.

She spent the rest of her life touring Europe and Canada, laying out her plans for freedom and equality, and collaborating with Europe's anti-fascist movements. Upon her death in 1940, her body was returned to Chicago, where she was buried beside leaders of the Haymarket labor riots.

EMI MAHMOUD

Migrated from Sudan via Yemen in 1998

Soon after her arrival in the States, Emi Mahmoud found herself in an English as a Second Language class struggling to say the word *apple*, because the *p* and *a* sounds were so different from her native Arabic. But fifteen years later, she was a college student at Yale with a full scholarship, studying molecular biology. As a senior, she defeated the world's best spoken-word performers to win the International World Poetry Slam Championship. Her winning poem, "Mama," which she wrote the morning of the contest, was infused with the history and weight of the ongoing violence in Darfur. Like her other poetry, it was written and performed in flawless English.

A line from a poem in her newest collection, *Sister's Entrance*, has since become the slogan for the UN Refugee Agency's "I Belong" campaign, raising support for stateless people. "Home is a question and every one of us, an answer," she wrote, though she attributes the sentiment to her grandmother.

Mahmoud sees her own life not as an expression of some of the struggles displacement and immigration can cause but as an experience that allows her to connect with diverse groups of people. "I'm the kid from Darfur, but I'm also a kid from Philly," she told Public Radio International. She says existing at the intersection of cultures has only broadened her platform, and it certainly seems to be the case: Not yet thirty, she can already count President Obama and the UN General Assembly among her poetry's audiences.

RECOMMENDED READING: POETRY COLLECTIONS

Language is the only homeland.

—CZESŁAW MIŁOSZ

CZESŁAW MIŁOSZ (POLAND/LITHUANIA)
New and Collected Poems 1931–2001

AÏDA TOURÉ (GABON)
Unmanifest Poems

BRYAN THAO WORRA (LAOS)
The Tuk-Tuk Diaries: My Dinner with Cluster Bombs

KHALED MATTAWA (LIBYA)
Zodiac of Echoes

JANINE JOSEPH (PHILIPPINES)
Driving Without a License

OCEAN VUONG (VIETNAM)
Night Sky with Exit Wounds

ACKNOWLEDGMENTS

MY DEEPEST GRATITUDE TO ALL THE PEOPLE WHO HAD A HAND IN this project:

Caitlin, without whom the idea for this book would not exist at all, and without whose skill and encouragement it wouldn't be half as good.

Emma, for your tireless research, spreadsheet expertise, and tiebreaking feedback.

Alison, for being the fastest and most flexible paintress known to this planet.

All the lovely folks at Random House who asked questions, sought answers, designed, edited, and otherwise helped to make this book a book.

Dionne, for sharing your history, which guided me to better understand the experience of enslaved people.

The journalists and biographers whose daily work shedding light on so many remarkable lives made this collection possible.

My talented friends and students, who remind me of the best parts about being a writer.

My family, for letting me whinge, and indulging me as I texted them newly unearthed facts at odd hours.

Zach, my favorite immigrant, for always supporting my work (and for sometimes making me stop working to go outside and eat pancakes).

To everyone featured in this book: Thank you for your bravery, intelligence, and perseverance, and for making this country a better place than it was when you found it.

—SARA

THIS HAS BEEN ONE OF THE MOST DEEPLY SATISFYING PROJECTS I'VE ever worked on—not least because of the talented, engaged, thoughtful people I got to work with. Sara amazed me with her instinct for the telling details that make a story come alive. Caitlin must be one of the most encouraging editors anywhere. Caitlin, Sara, and Emma were always quick with ideas, suggestions, and creative solutions, all informed by a clear sense of what this book could and should be.

I stand in awe of all the immigrants featured here. My own immigrant experience (an English speaker married to a U.S. citizen) was easy compared to most. Their stories confirm that this country has always renewed itself and grown in depth and richness through the gifts brought by those who arrived from somewhere else and made it their home.

—ALISON

COUNTRY INDEX

ABOUT THE AUTHOR

SARA NOVIĆ is the author of the novel *Girl at War* (2015), which won an American Library Association Alex Award and has been translated into thirteen languages. She has an MFA in Fiction and Literary Translation from Columbia University, and lives in Philadelphia.

sara-novic.com
Twitter: @NovicSara

ALISON KOLESAR grew up in Edinburgh, Scotland, and earned a history degree and a master's in art history before emigrating to the United States at the age of twenty-five. She has illustrated over a hundred books, drawing everything from people and plants to maps and machines.

alisonkolesar.com
Instagram: @alisonkolesar

ABOUT THE TYPE

This book was set in Fournier, a typeface named for Pierre-Simon Fournier (1712–68), the youngest son of a French printing family. He started out engraving wood-blocks and large capitals, then moved on to fonts of type. In 1736 he began his own foundry and made several important contributions in the field of type design; he is said to have cut 147 alphabets of his own creation. Fournier is probably best remembered as the designer of St. Augustine Ordinaire, a face that served as the model for the Monotype Corporation's Fournier, which was released in 1925.